Unlearning Marx

Why the Soviet failure was a triumph for Marx

T0154627

Unlearning Marx

Why the Soviet failure was a triumph for Marx

Steve Paxton

Winchester, UK
Washington, USA

JOHN HUNT PUBLISHING

First published by Zero Books, 2021
Zero Books is an imprint of John Hunt Publishing Ltd., No. 3 East St., Alresford,
Hampshire SO24 9EE, UK
office@jhpbooks.com
www.johnhuntpublishing.com
www.zero-books.net

For distributor details and how to order please visit the 'Ordering' section on our website.

ISBN: 978 1 78904 541 3
978 1 78904 542 0 (ebook)
Library of Congress Control Number: 2019956262

A CIP catalogue record for this book is available from the British Library.

Design: Stuart Davies

UK: Printed and bound by CPI Group (UK) Ltd, Croydon, CR0 4YY
US: Printed and bound by Thomson-Shore, 7300 West Joy Road, Dexter, MI 48130

We operate a distinctive and ethical publishing philosophy in
all areas of our business, from our global network of authors to
production and worldwide distribution.

Contents

Introduction – Why *Unlearning* Marx?

It's probably not uncommon for specialists in any field to feel that their subject is misunderstood by the public at large. Few people or ideas, though, can have been as consistently and grotesquely misrepresented as Karl Marx and historical materialism. There is nothing new in this – the right has always had a vested interest in misrepresenting Marx and his ideas – but the current propaganda campaign even outstrips the hysteria at the height of the cold war, if not in volume, then certainly in the level of absurdity. (One facet of this debate, the tendency to ascribe a random number of millions of deaths to the work of Marx, is so absurd that it ought not to have a place in any serious work, and yet such is its currency in contemporary dialogue that it can't be ignored. I've added an appendix to the end of this book to deal with this issue.) So the first sense in which we need to *unlearn* Marx is that as a society we need the idea of Marx to not induce a knee-jerk reaction based on misinformation. People don't need to agree with Marx, but it would help us all – and it would help the collective, society-wide conversation about where we're going – if more people had a reasonable notion of his ideas.

But this book is not just aimed at the right, or the casual observer who has heard fantastical tales. I think we on the left have some unlearning to do too. Many people, when discovering the world and finding their place in the political arena, observe the injustices of capitalism and are drawn to discover what alternatives might be out there. When they come across Marx it's almost always through the prism of the Soviet Union, and the work of Lenin and Trotsky. Stalin, everyone can agree, is not someone you want to set up as your mentor, but Lenin died before Stalin began his atrocities, and Trotsky was exiled and eventually murdered by Stalin's agents so they can safely be cleared of involvement in Stalin's excesses. Because of these historical circumstances, many people's introduction to Marx comes through what Lenin and Trotsky had to say about his work. This isn't necessarily the wrong way to read Marx, but neither is it the only way. Lenin and Trotsky were both caught up in a great social upheaval, and they were central characters in it. Of course, they read Marx from a different perspective to that which is available to us now. So one part of unlearning Marx is learning to forget what Lenin and Trotsky had to say and to try to read Marx without their help.

One of the consequences of the influence of Lenin and Trotsky is that many people come to Marx from a *political* perspective. They were primarily political actors, leading a great revolution and creating a new regime across a vast empire. This political angle is further enhanced because the first Marx that most people read is *The Communist Manifesto*. It's famous, it's short and it's less dense than a lot of Marx's other work. But it's not really what Marx was about. He and Engels were commissioned to write it. Engels wrote most of it and although it was heavily edited and rewritten by Marx the whole thing was a rush and it was produced as a reaction to the revolutions happening around them in Europe in 1848. It was a call to arms, a political pamphlet – the work of Marx the journalist rather than Marx the thinker. Marx's other widely known work is his three volume *Capital*. This analysis of the economic mechanisms of capitalism has provided the other central plank of Marxist thought, though it's too dense and too technical (and too repetitive) for the casual reader. While most approaches to Marx focus on the political polemics – as interpreted, developed and adapted by Lenin and Trotsky – or on the economics as laid out in *Capital*, here I want to focus on Marx's theory of history. For it is there, I will argue, that we find the most valuable lessons in terms of what Marx can teach us about where we are now, how we got here and where we're going next.

1. Marx, Socialism and the Soviet Union

1.1 Background

The theories of Karl Marx and the practical existence of the Soviet Union are inseparable in the public imagination, but for all the wrong reasons. The suggestion that the failure of the Soviet project provides favourable evidence in support of Marx's work is at least confusing for most, and beyond belief for others. And yet it's true. Not through some convoluted, revisionist, cherry-picking of odd fragments taken out of context, but just through reading what Marx actually wrote. When it comes to Marx and the Soviet Union, there's no shortage of well-worn, hand-me-down propaganda. But widespread belief doesn't make something true. The truth is this: Had the Soviets succeeded in building a socialist utopia, that news would have been welcomed by socialists, and no doubt by Marxists too, but it would have required conscientious Marxists to revise that allegiance, since such an outcome would have delivered a fatal blow to important Marxian[1] theses. Marx specifically predicted that projects like the Soviet Union would fail – not in a random moment of Nostradamus-like clairvoyance, but in detailed historical explanation, such that his whole approach to history would have been discredited had the Soviet Union succeeded in building a viable and genuinely socialist society.[2]

This book covers a lot of ground, and most of that ground has been the subject of extensive campaigns of misinformation, so the aim here is to establish a factual basis upon which to conduct an informed discussion of the subject matter, rather than the kangaroo court in which Marx is so often tried in his absence. The charge is relatively straightforward. The argument runs that the failure of the Soviet Union and various other attempts to create socialism illustrate that socialism can never work. That there is something inherent in socialist ideals that will inevitably

3

come into conflict with human nature and lead to collapse at best, mass murder at worst.

There are convincing arguments which the socialist can bring to bear against this charge, and these too are fairly straightforward – and indeed are compelling not just for socialists, but for many others who appreciate well-reasoned arguments and historical evidence. But there is also a set of specifically Marxian responses to the charge, based on Marx's approach to historical change. These responses go further than the socialist response because they set the argument in the context of a theory of history and allow us to develop an understanding of what the Soviet experience actually means in a world-historical context. Attempts to understand the Soviet experience from a Marxian perspective have largely focused on the concept of the USSR as an example of 'state capitalism'. The discussion of Marx's conception of capitalism in Part 2 will illustrate the fatal flaws with such an explanation. Other studies have focused on the economic structure in the Soviet period and centred around questions such as the relationship of the bureaucracy to the workers. This is a valuable approach, but one which I won't pursue here. Rather than addressing the exact nature of the Soviet economic structure, I'll examine the role of the Soviet Union in Marx's concept of historical change. The argument I present places some conceptual limitations on what the economic structure could be, but is not prescriptive on this matter in any but the broadest sense. It may be more accurate to say that in this context I'm inflexible only in terms of what the Soviet Union was not.

This book is set out in three main sections. The first covers the case against socialism and Marx (both cases are effectively the same), the respective defences (which are related but distinct) and a new, Marxian analysis of the meaning of the course of Russian and Soviet history. While this first section is designed to keep the argument flowing and accessible, such an approach is necessarily somewhat superficial and thus leaves the defence vulnerable to certain criticisms. As such, the second section provides a deeper analysis and discussion of the relevant Marxian concepts, while the third section contains a detailed account of Russian and Soviet history to support the claims made in Section One. Essentially, the second and third sections provide the evidence in support of the case made in the first section, with Section Two also shedding light on how we might usefully understand contemporary society from a Marxian perspective.

1.2 The Case Against Marx

In today's increasingly superficial political climate, right-wing commentators waste no time in labelling anything they don't like as 'Marxist' and associating Marxism with the atrocities of the Soviet gulags and thus whatever policy it is they're complaining about this week becomes an inevitable step towards the slaughter of tens of millions of innocents.[3] (Or sometimes it's hundreds of millions – when you're plucking figures from the air it's easy to add a zero or two.) Despite these hysterical claims, there is also a legitimate charge – that socialism has been tried and found wanting. It's a serious accusation, and as such must be addressed.[4]

It's clear that the Soviet Union wasn't a viable, socialist society. Not only did it ultimately fail, in that it ceased to exist, but even during its lifetime it suffered numerous problems. (That's not to say that there were no positive achievements, but few would argue that the Soviet experiment, overall, was a success.) The position of the right is that the reasons for the failure of the Soviet Union are not to be found in its specific historical circumstances, but in the very nature of socialism. To back this up, they cite any number of other self-proclaimed socialist experiments – those societies which used to be labelled *really-existing socialism*. In every case the establishment of 'socialism', they argue, has led to dictatorship, oppression, corruption, economic stagnation and social disintegration. The template is sufficiently established as to make it implausible to suggest that each instance was blighted by its own totally unique set of circumstances, unrelated to any of the others. There's a clear pattern of failure, the argument goes, and failure in a fairly routine way and there must be something behind this.

1.3 The Socialist Defence

The socialist defence against this charge is that there are sound, demonstrable reasons why the historical record does not show that socialism is unworkable, or that it inevitably leads to oppression and economic failure and so on. The argument is not that those self-proclaimed socialist countries were successful[5], it's that their failures were not failures of socialism, and they were not so in a particular set of non-inevitable ways.

Those asserting that history provides plentiful examples of socialist failure tend to include in their list almost any regime self-identifying as socialist[6]. Supporters of democracy are (correctly) never expected to justify or defend the undemocratic policies of the *Democratic People's Republic of Korea* or the *German Democratic Republic* (East Germany), and by the same token socialists should not be expected to defend the non-socialist policies of self-proclaimed socialist states.

As such, there's no merit in discussing here experiences such as that of Kampuchea under the Khmer Rouge. Their policies were virtually the opposite of socialism from the beginning (autarky, nationalism, racism), their demise was brought about by their defeat at the hands of the Socialist Republic of Vietnam, and in exile they were funded and armed to fight against 'socialist' Vietnam by the UK government of Margaret Thatcher and successive US administrations under presidents Carter, Reagan and Bush.[7]

It's not enough, though, for socialists to simply claim that no previous or current self-proclaimed socialist regimes were in fact practising or attempting genuine socialism. Aside from looking a bit too much like a 'no true Scotsman' defence, it's also vulnerable to two substantive criticisms.

1. That the historical record does show some instances of uncontroversially-socialist regimes, and
2. Where no evidence of socialist policies can be found, this may be because they are in fact impossible to implement, and as such they demonstrate that socialism is unworkable.

In answer to both of these points, socialists can concede that there are in fact some instances of genuine attempts to implement socialism, while still maintaining that the number and variety of such attempts remains insufficient to support a general conclusion that socialism will always, inevitably fail. Although it's easy for critics to run off a long list of failed 'socialist' states, the vast majority were actually territorial expansions of the Soviet Union, with puppet governments installed by Stalin right across Eastern Europe[8] and extensive Soviet influence in the Far East, South-East Asia and elsewhere[9]. Such was the extent of Soviet influence after the Second World War that all of the self-proclaimed 'socialist' states of that era received support – in cash, in infrastructure, in training, troops and weapons – from the Soviets. Obviously this backing didn't come without strings. Soviet support was accompanied by a requirement that the recipients model their regime in line with their sponsors.

What this means is that the supposed variety of failing socialist experiments actually amounts largely to a single experiment, attempted in a fairly limited range of circumstances. This in itself is enough to reduce the argument that there is sufficient historical evidence to demonstrate that socialism *cannot* work to an argument that Stalinist, Soviet socialism *did not* work.

One case, which cannot be laid at the door of Stalinism, is

the situation in the Soviet Union *before* Stalin came to power. It's not uncommon for socialists who disown Stalin to have a less critical view of both Lenin and Trotsky. There are, though, many contemporary reports of extensive repression in the first years after the revolution and critics are not slow to characterise such repression as an inevitable outcome of socialist ambitions. During this period, however, the revolutionary regime was not pursuing or even attempting to pursue socialist policies. Having extricated themselves from the First World War the regime was engulfed in a civil war with domestic counter-revolutionary forces, supported by states hostile to the revolution. The governments of the USA, UK, France, Japan, Canada, Australia, India and Italy sent troops straight from the battlefields of the First World War to fight against the revolution in Russia. This period was characterised not by attempts to establish socialism, but by policies devoted to a single aim – the survival of the revolutionary regime. Even Lenin conceded that 'everyone agrees that the immediate introduction of socialism in Russia is impossible'.[10] Even the apparently socialist programme of state procurement had been introduced by the Tsarist regime at the outbreak of the First World War, and was abandoned by the Bolsheviks as soon as the civil war had been won. Repression in the War Communism period cannot have been the result of socialist policies, since socialist policies were not pursued, or even attempted. It's more convincing to argue that the Bolshevik oppression during this period was really a continuation of the pre-revolutionary political culture in Russia, following the example of the tactics of the Tsarist *Okhrana*. Or, given what was going on elsewhere in the world, that early twentieth-century regimes often resorted to oppression, whatever their self-identified political position.

Other critics might argue that the very act of a revolutionary seizure of power will inevitably meet resistance from those who benefitted from the previous regime, and as such force – and likely excessive force and repression – is a predictable outcome of such swift and drastic change. This may well be the case, but it's a case about sudden revolution, not socialism. The capitalist revolutions of earlier centuries also met with resistance from those committed to the old order and Charles I and Louis XVI were not the only ones to have their heads parted from their bodies. All of these competing explanations of Bolshevik oppression hold more water than the charge that an ideology focused on helping to free the workers from oppression releases an inevitable instinct to persecute those very workers. Even if critics remain unconvinced by these arguments, it's clear that there *are* arguments to be made, and as such the trite dismissal of Marx 'because...history' is unworthy of serious thinkers.

As mentioned above, beyond these general arguments, there's a specifically Marxian explanation of the rise and fall of the Soviet Union, and it is to that which we now turn.

1.4 The Marxian Defence

I asserted above that had the Soviets succeeded in building a socialist utopia then such an outcome would have delivered a fatal blow to important Marxian theses. The reason for this is that Marx repeatedly insists that socialism can only be built as a product of mature capitalism, and Tsarist Russia did not provide any such foundation. This is not an abstract or isolated conditional requirement. Rather it is itself required by Marx's conception of historical change. Exactly how and why this all fits into Marx's overall theory of history is discussed in chapters 1.5 and 2.5, but for now we need only review his comments on the requirement that capitalism runs its course before a socialist revolution can succeed.

It comes as a surprise to many that Marx's view of capitalism was not entirely negative. Capitalism, he argued, is the only economic structure capable of developing productive capacity to a level sufficient to lift humankind from our historical situation of scarcity. Only capitalism can produce the material abundance required to set humanity free, developing the 'relentless productive forces of social labour...which alone can form the material base of a free human society'.[11] In *The German Ideology* Marx and Engels predicted failure for attempts to establish socialism before this material requirement had been met: 'this development of productive forces...is an absolutely necessary practical premise, because without it privation, *want* is merely made general, and with *want* the struggle for necessities would begin again, and all the old filthy business would necessarily be restored'.[12] Marx is warning that if you try to distribute resources fairly, when the total amount of resources is insufficient, you merely distribute shortfall to everyone, so that no one has enough ('want is merely made general' i.e. not-having-enough is extended to the whole population), the struggle for necessities ensues and we end up back with 'all the old filthy business'.

According to this approach, then, a free human society – communism – has a *material* precondition, a required level of development below which freedom (in the relevant sense) cannot be realised.[13] What Marx is saying here is that capitalism is uniquely suited to rapid development of productive capacity – that no other system can develop technology to the point where we can produce the material abundance required by a free society. Once capitalism has reached the limits of its potential to develop technology, then *and only then* will socialism be possible. Attempts to socialise in advance of this point will fail, he argues. Given that Russia in 1917 was one of the least advanced economies in Europe[14] it's clear that, according to Marx's theory of history, a socialist revolution there could not succeed. An attempt to build socialism on the basis of scarcity only leads to a more widespread distribution of that scarcity, and in 75 years – the blink of an eye in world-historical terms – the revolution collapses. Had the Soviet Union survived and gone on to produce a viable socialist society, then that would have embarrassed and discredited Marx's entire approach to historical change.

Why then, if it's so clear from Marx's work that a revolution in Russia in 1917 could not possibly succeed, did Marxist revolutionaries attempt just such a revolution? Well, it's fair to say they had been warned – the passages I've quoted above are only a small sample of the times Marx warns that a premature revolution cannot succeed. (In Chapter 1.5 we'll look further into Marx's theory of history and it will become clear why this is a necessary conclusion.) However, Marx did present a condition which, if met, could enable a premature socialist revolution to succeed, within the principles of his theory of history. Russian revolutionaries were becoming increasingly interested in Marx's work, particularly after the publication of a Russian translation of *Capital* in 1872. In 1881 Marx received a request, from Vera Zasulich,[15] to clarify his views 'on the possible fate of our rural commune, and on the theory that it is historically necessary for every country in the world to pass through all the phases of capitalist production'.[16] In his reply Marx rejects the idea that Russia may be able to skip the capitalist stage of development, stating that the peasant commune must 'be assured the normal conditions for spontaneous development'.[17]

The following year, though, Marx offered some hope to the Russian revolutionaries in the Preface to the 1882 second Russian edition of *The Communist Manifesto*. Here he posed the question at the centre of the Russian debates over his work: Could the Russian peasant commune 'pass directly into the higher form of communist common ownership? Or on the contrary, must it first pass through the same process of dissolution as constitutes the historical evolution of the West?' His answer provides a strict condition for such a possibility: 'The only answer to that possible today is this: If the Russian revolution becomes the signal for a proletarian revolution in the West, so that both complement each other, the present Russian common ownership of land may serve as the starting point for a communist development.'[18]

The condition is clear, and the assertion that a Russian revolution could only succeed if it was to precipitate revolutions in the most developed capitalist nations was not lost on Lenin or Trotsky. The Bolsheviks regarded a successful European proletarian revolution as absolutely necessary to the survival of a socialist regime in Russia. Lenin argued that following a proletarian revolution 'the only complete guarantee against restoration in Russia is a socialist revolution in the West. There is and can be no other guarantee.'[19] Trotsky was similarly committed to this position: 'Without the direct state support of the European proletariat the working class of Russia cannot remain in power.'[20] By acknowledging that the survival of a post-revolutionary regime in Russia would be dependent upon the direct state support of the European proletariat (itself requiring that successful socialist regimes had been established in the West), the Bolsheviks were able to advocate socialist revolution in Russia without rejecting Marx's theoretical approach to revolutionary change and historical development. Once in power, they set up the Comintern (Communist International) with the specific aim of precipitating proletarian revolutions in the advanced capitalist economies. Their failure to achieve this objective was finally conceded in 1943 when the Comintern was dissolved in favour of Stalin's (distinctly un-Marxist) policy of Socialism in One Country. Having failed to ignite revolutions in the advanced nations, the Soviet experiment could not, according to Marx, succeed in delivering a viable socialist society. Far from being disproved, Marx's work is vindicated by the Soviet failure to achieve socialism, and its eventual collapse.

1.5 The Marxian Counterclaim

Thus far we've established that Marx saw socialism as something only achievable *after* capitalism had fully developed, meaning that the Soviet experience represents supporting historical evidence for his approach, rather than an example of the failure of his ideas. That tells us something about Marx's theory of history, and something about what the Soviet Union wasn't, but it doesn't tell us much about what the Soviet Union actually was.

One of the problems with traditional interpretations of this matter is that everyone from any side has had a vested interest in adopting an interpretation which supports their political outlook. Having demonstrated that Marx bears no responsibility for the Soviet Union or its failure, we can take a step back and ask how Marx might have explained the rise and fall of the Soviet Union. In order to do this, we'll need to review some of the basic building blocks of Marx's theory of history. Here I'll provide only a short glossary of the main concepts. Further considerations and more technical discussion can be found in Section 2.[21]

Historical Materialism

Marx's theory of history – *Historical Materialism* – emphasises the importance of production and technology and asserts that in a general sense, the character of any social, political or cultural phenomenon is influenced by the prevailing economic structure, to a greater extent than vice versa. In the terminology of historical materialism, the material or economic *base* determines the character of the political, social and cultural *superstructure*.

This economic base can be further divided into two complementary aspects of production in any given historical setting:

The Productive Forces are essentially the material component of the productive process, composed of labour power and the means of production – raw materials, land, tools, machines, premises etc.

Production Relations are the social component of the productive process – they describe *who owns which productive forces*. A person may own their own labour power, or some or all of someone else's labour power. Or they may own or control any amount of means of production – a forest, a factory, a coal mine, an office building, a printing press and so on.[22] Production Relations simply describe who owns what.

In describing how production relations work in society, we can employ three further terms, *class*, *economic structure* and *revolution*:

A **class** is a group of people who share the same production relations. In general use the term *class* has many meanings – usually quite vague, and almost always encompassing social and cultural facets. In contrast, Historical Materialism uses the term to refer to groups such as slave, serf, proletarian and capitalist, each defined by its specific relations of production – its members' ownership or control of productive forces.

The **economic structure** is the sum of production relations in a society at a given time – that is, the classes of which a society is comprised. Capitalism, for example, is an economic structure in which most people are proletarians (free wage labourers), and most of the means of production are owned by the bourgeoisie (capitalists).

Revolution is the term given to the process of change whereby a society moves from one economic structure to another. Although some of Marx's political polemics occasionally call on workers to rise up and seize control of the means of production, there is nothing in historical materialism that requires any such event. A revolution doesn't have to involve manning the barricades or storming the Winter Palace. It's entirely possible for the revolutionary transition to occur peacefully. In fact, given the nature and time scale implicit in the concept of revolution in Historical Materialism, violence and unrest are more often the political repercussions of social upheavals created by the longer-term economic transformations which actually constitute the process of revolution.

The concept of revolution introduces the dimension of time

and the process of social change into the equation. How such change proceeds, and how revolutionary transformations come about can be described by the Development Thesis and the Primacy Thesis.

The Development Thesis and the Primacy Thesis

These twin theses form part of G.A. Cohen's rigorous treatment of the concepts of Historical Materialism in his ground-breaking and influential 1975 work *Karl Marx's Theory of History – A Defence*.[23]

The Development Thesis relates to technological development and states that *the productive forces tend to develop through history,* and that they will do so because humans are sufficiently intelligent to be able to improve their material situation, and sufficiently rational to be disposed to do so, given their historical situation of scarcity.

The Primacy Thesis states that *the nature of the production relations in a society is explained by the level of development of its productive forces* to a far greater extent than vice versa.[24] This means that the social aspect of the economic base (who owns what in a society) is determined by the material aspect – the level of technological development.

This claim is based on an assertion that as technology develops, different types of economic structure suit different levels of technological development. (A slave society might be suitable for building pyramids or keeping the Picts at bay, but it's not particularly conducive to the invention of spreadsheets or the development of ABS braking systems.)

Taken together the Development Thesis and the Primacy Thesis assert that:

- historical change is driven by technological development
- various economic structures arise and persist because they promote development

- as technology develops, an economic structure that had previously promoted development may now hinder further development
- in such a case, the economic structure will (eventually) give way and be replaced with a new economic structure which promotes further development. If economic structures sometimes impede further development, and if rationality dictates that development cannot be subverted indefinitely – then economic structures must 'rise and fall...as they enable or impede that growth'.[25]

The process of historical change in this context is similar to the evolutionary process of natural selection by chance variation. Throughout history there is constant experimentation with different ways of doing things. Not just in the development of new technologies but in the field of human relations. The variation of time, place and circumstance in the human experience has led to an incalculable number of combinations of production relations. Those experiments which favour further development at a time when existing relations are proving a drag on progress confer a productive advantage on their host societies. A productive advantage translates into a competitive edge for that society and, in the almost universal human situation of scarcity, a survival advantage. Over time, societies (or groups within a society) adopting production relations that 'work' will come to dominate their neighbours who resist such a change – a new economic structure emerges and the revolution is complete. Before we go on to look at Marx's treatment of the process whereby feudalism is transformed into capitalism, we should briefly review exactly what capitalism means in an historical materialist sense.

What is Capitalism?

In Marx's terms, capitalism is an economic structure in which the dominant production relation is that most workers are proletarians. The proletariat are defined by their ownership of their own labour power, and their non-ownership of any means of production. This means that:

- they are free in that they may sell their labour power on the open market to the highest bidder – they are not compelled to work for any particular capitalist
- they are unfree in that their non-ownership of any other means of production dictates that in order to live they *must* sell their labour power to some capitalist or other

This situation is in contrast to pre-capitalist labourers who were typically bound to the land by feudal obligations, unable to sell their labour power on the open market and compelled to labour for others, not by the need to earn their living, but by force, the threat of force or customary obligations. They were unfree in the sense that they didn't enjoy full ownership or control over their own labour power. Sometimes restrictions were formalised in their legal obligation to perform work for a feudal lord, in other cases the restrictions were less transparent, but no less real in terms of the lived experience of the worker. On the other hand, many workers enjoyed some rights over their means of subsistence – their obligations to their feudal lord may be partly reciprocated by provision of a plot of land on which they could grow crops and various rights of use or access to communal assets – the right to graze livestock on a common or to collect firewood from a spinney for example. Capitalism sweeps away both the rights and the obligations of the workers.

Under capitalism then, most people are proletarians, who own no means of production. A much smaller class are the capitalists – or bourgeoisie – who own most of the means of production. Full membership of the bourgeoisie is defined by ownership of sufficient means of production as to not need to work in order to be able to live. A bourgeois industrialist or landowner *may* actually work, but their class location requires only that they *need not* do so. These are of course ideal-typical definitions, and in capitalism, as in any system, numerous shades and intermediate classes exist. Section Two includes discussion of some intermediate classes under capitalism, among a number of other concepts of Historical Materialist theory.

So how do these two classes – the proletariat and the bourgeoisie – come into being? How do they emerge from the feudal system in which workers are not free in the way that proletarians are, but also whose unfreedom is a product of customary power relations, rather than of economic necessity? How are feudal barons usurped by capitalists as owners of the means of production? How are the means of production themselves transformed into capital – from the 'individualised and scattered means of production into socially concentrated ones, [from] the pygmy property of the many into the huge property of the few'?[26]

The Transition from Feudalism to Capitalism – The Bourgeois Revolution

Just as Marx argues that a condition of sufficient technological development must be met for a successful socialist revolution, he also asserts a similar condition exists for a successful bourgeois revolution:

> the overthrow of the absolute monarchy would be merely temporary if the economic conditions for the rule of the bourgeois class had not yet become ripe. Men build a new world for themselves, not from the 'treasures of this earth', as grobian superstition imagines, but from the historical achievements of their declining world. In the course of their development they first have to produce the material conditions of a new society itself, and no exertion of mind or will can free them from this fate.[27]

With 75 per cent of the working population of England engaged in agriculture at the start of the sixteenth-century, each worker was producing enough for themselves and one-third of another person. This level of productivity is simply not enough to enable urbanisation or industrialisation on any significant scale.[28] With a finite amount of usable farmland it would be necessary to improve output per acre and also output per worker. Before any kind of industrial revolution could take place, there would need to be a revolution in agricultural productivity. The technological developments enabling this *agricultural revolution* could get only so far within the existing economic structure, and then feudal relations of production began to hamper further progress. During the Tudor period workers were increasingly turfed off the land through a series of measures adopted by progressive landowners, beginning to favour profit from farming over rent from tenants. As the Tudors gave way to the Stuarts the progressive farmers and emerging merchant class used their economic power to wrest political power from the Crown and into the hands of their representatives in Parliament. (The economic power of the rising capitalist class was such that they were able to consolidate political power even to the extent of chasing out James II and replacing him with the more compliant William of Orange – James' nephew and son-in-law – as a constitutional monarch, answerable to Parliament.) From this point the forcible evictions of workers accelerated under the legal mechanism of *Parliamentary Enclosure* until almost 9 million acres had been redistributed from small-scale, subsistence workers to capitalist landowners by 1850, creating an army of landless poor who had no choice but to head for the developing towns in search of wage labour.[29]

Marx repeatedly emphasises the importance of the creation of a proletariat in the process of bourgeois revolution: 'the capitalist mode of production and of accumulation, and therefore capitalist private property, have for their fundamental condition the annihilation of self-earned private property; in other words, the expropriation of the labourer'.[30] The creation of capital, 'the transformation of the individualised and scattered means of production into socially concentrated ones, of the pygmy property of the many into the huge property of the few' accompanies the 'expropriation of the great mass of the people from the soil, from the means of subsistence, and from the means of labour' and forms the 'prelude to the history of capital'.[31]

Marx's analysis of the development of capitalism in England emphasises the role of technological development, leading to a shift in production relations which in turn enabled further developments and more shifts in production relations until the economic power had come to lie with the emerging capitalist class, leading eventually to conflict as they assumed political power.[32] The economic foundations of the old order had crumbled in the face of technological developments and the rise of the bourgeoisie. But there was no great revolutionary moment where the traditional aristocracy were swept away by the upstart capitalists. Although there had been bloodshed in the civil wars it mainly resulted from the inability of sections of the old order to embrace the changing world. There was a social, cultural and emotional investment in the traditional way of doing things which they couldn't forego – at least, not without a fight. As for the emerging capitalists – they were largely drawn from the lower and middle ranks of the feudal establishment. The crucial revolutionary transformation was in the ownership relations – in the development of new class locations, rather than in the personnel occupying certain positions in the economic structure. Far from the capitalist upstarts putting the old feudal barons to the sword, the brunt of the suffering was borne by the workers – evicted from the land, subjected to persecution, forced to seek wage labour in the emerging industrial economy and drafted into service to be killed and maimed in the civil wars on both sides, though neither side was fighting for their interests. In Marx's words:

> Thus were the agricultural people, first forcibly expropriated from the soil, driven from their homes, turned into vagabonds, and then whipped, branded, tortured by laws grotesquely terrible, into the discipline necessary for the wage system.[33]

He lists numerous Acts of the sixteenth and seventeenth centuries specifying punishments including whipping, branding (variously on the breast, back, shoulder or forehead, depending on the 'crime'), cutting off half an ear, abduction of the transgressor's children into slavery, use of irons and manacles, imprisonment, slavery and execution.

The transition from feudalism to capitalism, then, has a material precondition – a level of technological development sufficient to enable urbanisation and industrialisation – and consists of a number of essential processes:

- The dissolution of feudal obligations
- The expropriation of the immediate producers
- The concentration of the means of production

Marx also notes that aspects of the transition may be accompanied by violence and brute force, but that these would likely be directed at the workers, rather than the representatives of the old order. He further notes that the state may play a role in assisting the bourgeoisie's rise to power, and that amid the turmoil and chaos, the workers may be able to organise sufficiently to snatch political power, but that:

> its victory will only be temporary, only an element in the service of the bourgeois revolution itself, as in the year 1794, as long as in the course of history, in its 'movement', the material conditions have not yet been created which make

necessary the abolition of the bourgeois mode of production and therefore also the definitive overthrow of the political rule of the bourgeoisie. The terror in France could thus by its mighty hammer-blows only serve to spirit away, as it were, the ruins of feudalism from French soil.[34]

1.6 From Feudalism to Capitalism in Russia

We noted above that the assessment of Russia in 1917 as not being the most advanced capitalist nation was so uncontroversial as not to require specific empirical support. Now though, I want to make two further claims which *will* need supporting evidence. Those claims are, firstly, that by 1917 Russia had not even entered a capitalist phase, and secondly, that by 1917 capitalism could not have existed in Russia because the necessary preconditions were not in place. The required supporting evidence for these claims will come later,[35] but for now we should note that if Russia was not capitalist – and *could not be* capitalist – in 1917 and is capitalist now, then what happened in between (i.e. the rise and fall of the Soviet Union) must have included the processes that make capitalism possible, and as such must constitute some or all of Russia's transition from feudalism to capitalism – Russia's bourgeois revolution – regardless of any political ideology espoused by the Soviets during this period. Of course, I'm not claiming that the Soviet regime *wanted* to put in place the foundations of capitalism, far from it. But the Soviet regime was hardly ever in a position to do what it wanted anyway. As Alec Nove has commented, 'real life at no time conformed to the government's intentions'.[36]

Pre-revolutionary Russia

Before we look at the course of Soviet history, we need to examine briefly the last decades of the Tsarist regime. The feudal system in Russia formally came to an end with the emancipation of the serfs through a series of measures in the 1860s, meeting the first

1. Marx, Socialism and the Soviet Union

of our three essential processes of the bourgeois revolution – the dissolution of feudal obligations. The terms of the emancipation, though, did not create a proletariat in Russia, or even a class of independent peasants, as had been the case in most of Western Europe. Former serfs received allocations of land, but they didn't enjoy full ownership rights over such land. In addition to obligatory redemption payments owed on this land, the peasant commune (or *Mir*) remained an important influence on rural landholding. Most land was held in common with other commune members and the commune would periodically repartition land to its member households. The survival of the commune placed a number of limitations on the development of capitalist agriculture, not only preventing the utilisation of available technology, but also restricting the development of capitalist ownership relations. By 1917 the Russian peasantry no longer laboured under a feudal yoke, but remained tied to the soil through a number of customary arrangements. Capitalism could not develop until the peasantry had been dispossessed of any sense of ownership or entitlement to the land. Even by 1917 capitalist production relations had penetrated the lives of no more than 10 per cent of Russian workers and peasants. The vast majority of immediate producers fell outside of our conception of proletarian status, either by virtue of their possession of relevantly significant means of production or because of their insufficient control over their own labour power.

The backward nature of Russian agriculture also limited the potential for urban growth and industrialisation on any significant scale. In 1905 nearly three-quarters of Russian workers gave their main occupation as agriculture, fishing, hunting or lumbering.[37] With the peasantry held back by the regulations and common ownership of the *Mir*, there wasn't much encouragement for development from the landowning gentry and nobility either. Edelman observes that 'most Russian landlords actually knew little about agronomy, food processing or animal husbandry. They lacked the necessary capital and the majority of them still considered service, not farming, to be their true career.'[38] At around 700 kg/ha, arable productivity in Russia in 1913 was lower than that attained in England by 1600.[39]

Industry stumbled along, chiefly sponsored by the state or foreign capital – the absence of a proletariat in Tsarist Russia was matched by the weakness of the bourgeoisie. Walkin argues that 'Russia did not develop a middle class similar to the powerful middle classes of the west. Those concerned with trade and industry were small in number, largely illiterate until the end of the nineteenth century, and dependent on the state.'[40] The state did become involved in trying to stimulate industrial development but was hindered by the absence of the final two of the three conditions Marx considers necessary for the development of capitalism: the expropriation of the peasantry from the soil, and the concentration of the means of production into capital. If either of these conditions were to be met, the Russian economy would also need to modernise considerably in order to be able to provide sufficient output to achieve the material development Marx asserts is an essential pre-requisite for capitalist development.

With no significant proletariat or bourgeoisie, without efficient agriculture or established industry, not only was Russia in 1917 too backward for a proletarian leap into socialism, but hadn't even met the required conditions for a bourgeois revolution into capitalism. Furthermore the capacity for the required technological development to facilitate such a revolution simply was not there. As we've already noted, the Bolshevik leadership agreed with Marx that their revolution could only survive if it proved to be the trigger for revolutions in the more advanced capitalist nations. Even in ideal circumstances building socialism would have had to take a back seat while the regime concentrated on domestic survival and precipitating international revolution. This was even more so in the far from ideal circumstances in which the Bolsheviks found themselves in the immediate aftermath of their seizure of power.

The Soviet Era

The first task of the regime was to extricate the country from the First World War; it was then almost immediately attacked on all sides by domestic and foreign enemies in a series of civil wars in which the counter-revolutionaries enjoyed support from Western governments. This period of 'War Communism' saw the Bolsheviks marshalling all resources into the achievement of the single aim of survival. There was no other priority. Having emerged somehow victorious from this series of conflicts by the beginning of 1921, the Bolsheviks now had the opportunity to embark on a peacetime programme of reform. The implementation of socialist policies, though, would have to wait. The chaos of war, revolution and more war had exacerbated the already poor productive output of the economy and the Bolsheviks were in no position to start directing the distribution of already insufficient resources. The regime had little option but to accept concessions to the market, under a set of measures known as the New Economic Policy (NEP). The wartime policy of grain requisitioning (inherited from the pre-revolutionary war effort) was replaced with a tax-in-kind, and later with a money tax. The sale of peasant land and the hiring of agricultural labour became lawful. A private sector was encouraged in industry and retail. The Soviets were stabilising the regime and consolidating their position, but modernisation was slow and the prospect of socialism or of revolutions in the West was receding all the time.

The Soviet leadership debated whether to leave the NEP in place, risking extended attachment to – and dependence on – the market, or to increase the pace of modernisation by focusing resources on heavy industry. The second option would sacrifice peasant and worker consumption to industrial investment, as the price of overcoming Russia's backwardness

– in Preobrazhensky's words, the state would buy cheap grain from the peasants and sell expensive food to the housewife.[41] Neither War Communism nor the NEP had moved the Soviet economy any closer to socialism.

Although Lenin had begun to show concern over the strength of the market as early as 1922, it was only after his death, and after Stalin's rise to power, that the decision to abandon NEP was firmly set. Even as late as 1927, on the eve of the planned start date for the first Five-Year Plan, Stalin's rhetoric emphasised gradual change, brought about by example and persuasion rather than force or pressure. By the end of 1929, though, having eliminated his opposition and assumed full control of the Soviet Union, the targets of the first Five-Year Plan were revised upwards, accompanied by brutal methods of requisitioning and forced collectivisation.

While the organisation of the Five-Year Plans and collectivisation through state planning may have had acceptably socialist credentials, the end result – the expropriation of the peasantry and the concentration of their scattered plots into large-scale farms – is right out of Marx's list of pre-requisites for the development of capitalism – expropriating the peasants from the land, and consolidating their property into modern large-scale farms. Furthermore the harsh methods of their implementation look very much like the grim realities of the equivalent process in Western Europe a few centuries earlier, which enabled the birth of capitalism and the acceleration of urbanisation and industrialisation.

By the time of Stalin's death in 1953 the economic conditions laid out by Marx as pre-requisites for the development of capitalism were all in place. Feudal bonds had been dissolved formally in the nineteenth century and in practice by the Bolsheviks under the NEP. The peasants had been forcibly expropriated from the land – their conception of ownership had been broken by collectivisation, and would soon be a distant memory. The land had been transformed from the scattered and divided property of the peasantry into huge collective farms (*kolkhoz*) and state farms (*sovkhoz*), making the land ripe for conversion to capital a few generations later, as well as enabling some degree of mechanisation of agriculture. The increased yields resulting from mechanisation enabled large-scale industrialisation and urbanisation, providing the material precondition for capitalism. All that was required now was the transfer of assets from the state into private hands.

As we noted earlier, a central claim of historical materialism is that any given economic structure may promote development at a certain stage, but eventually will become a hindrance to further growth. The Soviet system had proved itself able to promote development from an immediately post-feudal level to that required for the emergence of a fully capitalist economy. But by the post-Stalin era the USSR found itself up against the advanced capitalist economies of the West, with which it could not compete. Western economies were reaching a level of development which was impossible within the Soviet model. While the Soviets could – in the short term – compete in terms of state-sponsored projects such as space exploration, the technology of the emerging digital age was led by consumer demand, and the Gosplanners could not hope to compete with the invisible hand of the market. The failure to meet consumer demand created a channel of internal disquiet aimed at the Soviet regime, alongside demands for religious freedom and resurgent nationalism. (Remember that the Soviet Union inherited the territory of the Russian Empire – only half the population were Russian nationals and the population of the USSR was drawn from over 100 nationalities. Of these, 22 had more than a million members in the 1989 census, and 15 had their own republics within the USSR.) Internal tensions exacerbated the external pressures of the Cold War, which even in its later stages was a major drain on Soviet resources. As the regime wavered and debated over whether to adopt reforms along Swedish or Hungarian lines, prominent members of the establishment were positioning themselves to take advantage of the inevitable shift to private ownership. When privatisation came, these well-placed members of the Soviet bureaucracy – the *Nomenklatura* – took full advantage, subverting the various schemes aimed at distributing wealth and resources among the citizenry and creating a de facto class of capitalist oligarchs. Amid this process the Soviet Union was dissolved and political power passed to an ostensibly democratic system of government which few imagine serves the needs of anyone who doesn't own at least a coalfield or two.

So we can see that the course of Russian history has followed the path expected by historical materialist theory, despite some confusion caused by the 75-year interregnum under a regime claiming to be socialist, and under Stalin's policy of Socialism in One Country claiming to have subverted Marx's predictions and leapt over capitalism into communism. From a feudal economic structure before the emancipation of the serfs in the 1860s to a capitalist economic structure by the end of the twentieth century, Russia passed through exactly the processes Marx identified as central to England's transformation a few centuries earlier.

Economic Determinism in Historical Materialism

A criticism often levelled at historical materialism is that it is a form of economic determinism. The argument runs that it crudely reduces all human interactions to their economic aspect. I think the explanation of Russian history given above provides a good illustration of the way in which economic factors are held to be fundamentally drivers of change, but are not considered to be all-encompassing in determining the exact course of history. It's worth reviewing our earlier summary of the process of historical change:

- historical change is driven by technological development

- various economic structures arise and persist because they promote development
- as technology develops, an economic structure that had previously promoted development may now hinder further development
- in such a case, the economic structure will (eventually) give way, and be replaced with a new economic structure which promotes further development. If economic structures sometimes impede further development, and if rationality dictates that development cannot be subverted indefinitely – then economic structures must 'rise and fall...as they enable or impede that growth'.[42]

The only really *deterministic* proposal here is that development cannot be subverted indefinitely, which arises simply from the assertion of the development thesis that humans are sufficiently ingenious as to be able to improve their lives, and sufficiently rational as to not reject the opportunity to do so (temporary bouts of irrationally rejecting progress for religious or other cultural reasons notwithstanding).

Obviously historical materialism doesn't predict or dictate the actual events by which this process will manifest itself. In the case of Russia, had Nicholas II been less incompetent or his cousin Archduke Michael been less cowardly perhaps Tsarism may have persisted and overseen a transition to capitalism (though it's unlikely that it would have survived the transition unless the Romanovs could find it in themselves to embrace a constitutionally limited role). Had the Provisional Government enjoyed better leadership, then perhaps after the Great War Russia could have overcome its past and its backwardness and embarked on a gradual path to capitalism. Had Lenin lived longer, or Stalin been thwarted in his ambitions perhaps a continuation of NEP into more conciliatory Five-Year Plans may have prepared the ground for capitalism through a less traumatic twentieth century. (Though this would certainly have weakened the Soviet position against Hitler's invasion in the Second World War.) Perhaps, without Soviet direction, Russia would have failed to develop the preconditions for capitalism and become imperially or commercially subjugated to the advanced Western powers. Or perhaps a typical proto-bourgeois middle class may have developed and set in motion a more traditional bourgeois revolution. One way or another, capitalism was coming to Russia. As it happens, Russia's bourgeois revolution was carried out largely by the Soviet regime's pursuit of survival and modernisation.

The argument I have presented here relies on a view of the Soviet Union as a transitional economic structure, following on from the dissolution of feudalism and preparing the way for capitalism. This concept of a transitional structure is not one that received a lot of attention from Marx or writers in the historical materialist tradition and given that we are probably entering a transitional phase as I write, that is perhaps a deficiency which needs correcting. I've made some progress to that end in Section Two.[43]

It's been my intention in this section to be as succinct as possible in order to keep the argument flowing and to avoid getting too bogged down with supporting evidence or distracted by qualifications or counter-arguments. While this approach makes it easier to get the gist of the argument across, it's also unavoidably superficial, leaving the case I've made open to certain criticisms or disputes. The following two sections address this matter by providing a deeper level of discussion about the concepts employed and a body of supporting evidence for the claims made. Section Three consists of a documented analysis of the relevant factors of Russian and Soviet history but first, Section Two provides a deeper analysis of the concepts of historical materialist theory and addresses some potential criticisms.

2. Deeper into Marx

2.1 Introduction

The main aim of this section is to expand our discussion of the concepts of historical materialism in the context of providing supporting information for the arguments made in Section One. A further aim is to put some meat on the theoretical bones of Section One in a general sense, because it's never a bad idea to think carefully about difficult concepts, or to explore ideas and their applicability to the real world.

Our discussion on the concept of class, for example, may help us to determine the size of the proletariat in pre-revolutionary Russia (which in turn helps us to evaluate the contention that capitalism was largely absent from that society). An analysis of the theory of class may also help us to understand how we might apply Marxian concepts to our current experiences. Although a Marxian class analysis of modern Western society is beyond the scope of this book, it's worth bearing in mind as we discuss the abstract concepts just how this framework might inform an approach to contemporary issues. What is the class status of drivers working for *Uber* or *Deliveroo* for example? Are they proletarians, or does their ownership of their own means of transport make them part of the petty-bourgeoisie? Are there parallels between their situation and that of a nineteenth-century weaver under the putting-out system? At times, as we delve deeper into questions like these it can start to feel like there's nothing useful in whatever answers we arrive at – like the whole thing is an academic exercise with no relevance to the real world. In fact, though, these are important questions because locating someone in the economic structure based on the extent and type of their ownership of the means of production tells us a lot about how different structural changes might be received by them. For example, there are a growing number of workers in this position of *disguised employment* – effectively employed but having none of the benefits of a full-time position and what's more, having to buy and maintain their own tools of the trade. If these workers feel like they are really employees, but stripped of some of the benefits that were won by their predecessors, they're less likely to feel like they have a stake in society than if they regard themselves as petty-bourgeois proprietors on the first rung of the entrepreneurial ladder. As such, their reaction to an idea like Universal Basic Income – essentially the acceptance that we *all* deserve a share of the spoils of progress – is likely to be more positive if they feel that they have until now been denied their rightful dividend than if they feel that they already have a stake in society and don't want to see it distributed to others. Aggregating the various class locations of our current populations might also help us to understand where we are as a society – are we still in the midst of the capitalist epoch, or are there signs that we've entered a transitional stage away from capitalism?

Hopefully, keeping such questions in mind will help to ground the necessarily theoretical nature of the discussions around abstract concepts such as class, economic structures and modes of production.

2.2 Class

The notion of class is central to Marx's work, yet he never provided an explicit, unified definition of exactly what he meant by the term. Although he can't escape the charges of ambiguity, which have led to fierce debates concerning the 'real' Marxian *meaning* of class, it is possible to draw out an approach to this problem which is both consistent with Marx's most frequent use of the concept and sensitive to the broader theoretical claims of historical materialism.

Class Consciousness

An important question in any attempt to construct a Marxian definition of class is that concerning the role of consciousness. This concept permeates into wider Marxian ideas, such as the nature of revolution and the process of historical change. E.P. Thompson suggests that:

> When we speak of *a* class we are thinking of a very loosely defined body of people who share the same categories of interests, social experiences, traditions and value-system, who have a *disposition to behave* as a class, to define themselves in their actions and in their consciousness in relation to other groups of people in class ways. But class itself is not a thing, it is a happening.[44]

In itself this is a perfectly reasonable statement of Thompson's handling of the term 'class'. His attempt to recruit Marx to this position, though, is more problematic.[45] The criteria which Thompson requires in order that class may be said to have 'happened' is at once more demanding and more vague than is either necessary or useful in assessing Marx's uses of the concept of class. It is true that Marx sometimes suggested that 'a disposition to behave as a class' figures in the criteria by which a group of people can be termed a class. The most notable case is that of the French peasantry in *The Eighteenth Brumaire of Louis Bonaparte*:

> Insofar as millions of families live under economic conditions of existence that separate their mode of life, their interests and their culture from those of the other classes, and put them in hostile opposition to the latter, they form a class. Insofar as there is only a local interconnection among these small landholding peasants, and the identity of their interests beget no community, no national bond and no political

organization among them, they do not form a class.[46]

Here Marx lists community, national bond and political organisation as elements essential to the definition of class. Yet he notes their absence in the lives of the French peasantry[47]*and* in the same work refers to that group as a class.[48]

The apparent confusion, though, is resolved in *The Eighteenth Brumaire* when Marx makes the distinction between a 'class-in-itself' and a 'class-for-itself'.[49] The French peasantry, by virtue of shared 'conditions of economic existence', constitutes a class-in-itself, but, lacking in community, national bond and political organisation, it cannot be considered as a class-for-itself. This is Marx's distinction between a class defined by shared relations of production, and a class whose members have *recognised their shared interest* in the light of that shared situation.

An intermediate position was identified by Marx in *The Poverty of Philosophy* with respect to the English working class. More than an objectively observable class-in-itself, but still not a conscious class-for-itself, the working class had become 'a class as against capital'[50] (that is, it had attained a collective existence for others, before attaining a consciousness 'for itself'.)[51] Although the present discussion is concerned with the role of consciousness in a *definition* of class, it is helpful at this point to briefly consider what role consciousness is expected to play in a *theory* of class. It is commonly supposed that historical materialism is committed to a theory of class in which class location must always create a class consciousness which *explains* the actions of the members of that class. Nicos Poulantzas, for example, argues that, 'For Marxism, social classes involve in one and the same process both class contradictions and class struggle; social classes do not firstly exist as such and only then enter into a class struggle... Classes exist only in the class struggle.'[52] Yet it is implausible to suggest that Marx thought that every group which he called a class existed in the strong sense of a fully conscious, actively and collectively 'engaged' class-for-itself.[53] Thus a Marxian definition of class must be capable of identifying a class-in-itself as well as a class-for-itself. Class-consciousness is a property which is present in the latter but not the former 'type' of class (i.e. it is a property which classes may or may not possess) and as such it cannot be considered as a component in a general Marxian definition of class. Yet a Marxian theory of class does require that there is some relationship between class location and revolutionary action. That relationship is here conceived to be one in which the features of an individual's class location (within the network of production relations) are such that under certain circumstances a revolutionary course of action becomes a rational option for that individual (and thus for other individuals who share that class location).[54]

Several further points should be noted here. First, it is important to recognise that the potential for revolutionary action outlined above is not a necessary feature of all class locations. Marx never predicted a necessary revolutionary role for the petty-bourgeoisie, for example. Nor did he consider the fall of slavery (in the ancient world or in the southern states of North America) to have been effected by a class-conscious slave population.

Second, it is also necessary to understand that a 'revolutionary course of action' does not always involve commandeering the Smolny Institute or storming the Bastille. For Marx, the 'era of social revolution' is essentially characterised by the displacement of one dominant production relation by another. It is possible that this revolution could consist entirely of processes of 'adaptive metamorphosis' or revolution from above. Indeed, Marx's description of the emergence of capitalism in England includes elements of both of these processes. He describes how 'the great feudal lords created an incomparably larger proletariat by the driving of the peasantry from the land'[55]and how they then 'vindicated for themselves the rights of modern private property in estates to which they had only a feudal title'.[56] In this way the feudal landowners were able to deliver 'what the capitalist system demanded...a degraded and almost servile condition of the mass of the people, the transformation of them into mercenaries and of their means of labour into capital'.[57] Thus the bourgeois revolution is carried through, in part at least, by the actions of members of the feudal class in transforming themselves into members of the bourgeoisie (placing their operations on a capitalist basis), and, in the process, transforming the peasantry into a proletariat; free from feudal obligations and 'free from, unencumbered by, any means of production of their own'.[58] Although he sometimes refers to the English civil war and the 'Glorious Revolution' as focal points in the transition from feudalism to capitalism, Marx clearly views that transition as a process rather than a 'moment'. He saw the bourgeois revolution in England as involving a variety of forms of revolutionary action, and a broad range of 'revolutionaries', including feudal landowners.

Finally, it is necessary to distinguish between maximum and minimum forms of 'collective class consciousness'. The maximum form is that in which a substantial proportion of the members of a class perceive their own interests to be broadly the same as the interests of the class as a whole, and recognise other classes whose interests are antagonistic to their own. The minimum form of collective class consciousness may be present when members of a class act in a revolutionary manner, not through recognition of collective class interests, but as individuals motivated independently of each other by the conditions of their class location in relation to the prevailing historical situation. Agents may act with a degree of uniformity (because they share the same structural conditions of existence), without necessarily experiencing any sense of solidarity. Historical materialism requires that revolutionary action is collective action and that it is derived from the experiences created by class location, but it does not require that it is so derived via a manifestation of the maximum form of class consciousness.

If, then, classes may be defined independently of considerations relating to the presence (or absence) of class consciousness, what factors are to be considered as contributing to a Marxian definition of class?

Defining Classes

Jon Elster notes that, 'The view most frequently attributed to Marx is that a class is a group of persons who stand in the same relation of property or non-property to the factors of production, i.e. labour-power and the means of production.' Elster argues against the practice of defining classes strictly in terms of 'relations of property or non-property to the factors of production'. He suggests that 'property and non-property are too crude as indicators of class membership' and notes that 'Marx warns against any attempt to define classes in terms of the *kind* or *amount* of property owned.'[59] But Marx was concerned to avoid the absurd situation in which *every* different kind and amount of property could be taken to indicate a different class, giving rise to an 'infinite fragmentation' of classes. But it is not the kinds and amounts of *property* that we argue should be the defining factors, but the kinds and amounts of *ownership*. In this light, property and non-property may be rescued from the status of 'crude indicators' and form the basis of a more sophisticated approach to class than that envisioned by Elster. The 'ownership' approach is bluntly asserted by Cohen: 'A person's class is established by nothing but his objective place in the network of ownership relations, however difficult it may be to identify such places neatly.'[60] The context of this statement allows that 'ownership relations' may be defined as relations of effective control by persons over productive forces or other persons, and that the sum of these relations may be termed the 'economic structure'.

This means of identifying class locations can be thought of as the *basic structural definition* of class. Attempts to apply such a definition of class to actual historical situations have indeed proved difficult and different theorists have applied various supplementary or mediating criteria in order to facilitate this task. It's useful to distinguish between those which offer *mediating* criteria and those which offer *supplementary* criteria, for as we will see, the former turn out to be far more useful and robust than the latter. Mediating criteria are those factors which are directly determined by relations of production. Supplementary criteria are those which introduce factors which are not determined by structural conditions, and thus concede that production relations alone are not sufficient to establish a viable definition of class. The distinction may be illustrated by examining Cohen's treatment of two factors which bear upon the definition of the proletariat.

Cohen argues that non-ownership of any means of production 'is not as essential to proletarian status as is traditionally maintained'.[61] He provides examples from the early American garment industry and refers to Marx's treatment of a weaver under the putting-out system. Each of these workers 'owns' some of the means of production which he uses, but Cohen offers two reasons why they should be characterised as proletarians. The first reason is that their ownership of some means of production is not sufficient for them to escape the economic compulsion to sell their labour power to another. Secondly, their ownership of means of production is adventitious: 'The capitalist is able to supply the machine, and if it suited him he would do so. If he abstains from owning it, that is because it benefits him not to.'[62] These producers all 'enjoy' what Marx termed the 'illusion of ownership'.[63] The arrangement simply shifts the burden of ownership to the worker, who now becomes responsible for repairs, maintenance and replacement of consumable parts – and must own and maintain the equipment even in times of little or no demand for work. Another burden is that the worker, having now invested in the machinery or other 'tools of the trade' (and likely with payments to keep up), has less flexibility in terms of changing occupations. These considerations are not anachronisms, suited only to the industrial proletariat of the Victorian era. Similar questions could now be asked of occupations emerging in the gig economy and in industries dominated by disguised employment. This refinement of the traditional definition of proletarian status is compatible with the *basic structural definition* of class as it is framed in terms which are directly derived from structural conditions. The proletarian may still be identified by virtue of the extent and nature of his effective control over productive forces.

Elsewhere, though, Cohen introduces the criteria of subordination into the definition of the proletariat, arguing that the structural characterisation of proletarian status applies only within the set of subordinated producers. This is necessitated, he argues, by the presence of individuals whose basic structural class location is the same as that of the proletariat, yet who are manifestly not proletarians. He cites the example of 'top-salaried architects' who 'need not own the tools of their trade, but...are not proletarians',[64] though the situation applies similarly to any well-paid technical or managerial position. Under capitalism, though, the subordination/domination axis does not describe a relation of production and must be seen as supplementary to the basic structural definition unless it can be shown that an individual's place on that axis derives directly from his location within the network of production relations.[65] This means that if we have to accept that the degree of subordination is a factor in defining an individual's class location, then we must also accept that a purely structural approach is not sufficient.

Cohen asserts that the proletarian's subordination ensues because his lack of means of production forces him to contract with a capitalist on terms which effect that subordination. But

I think Cohen is wrong here. The proletarian's subordination cannot be said to derive directly from the structural conditions of his existence if some individuals who share those conditions are deemed not to be subordinated. Given that the reasoning which links the proletarian's structural location to his subordination is theoretically and intuitively sound,[66] this discrepancy can only be resolved if workers such as the top-salaried architect can be shown to occupy a different structural location to the proletarian.

One way of approaching this problem is to pose the question: 'how do architects (and other professionals) gain non-subordinate employment from a position which appears to be structurally equivalent to that of the proletarian, who can (usually) only gain subordinate employment and who is generally thus restricted *because* of his structural position?' The answer to this question lies in the professional's superior bargaining position in the labour market, which derives from his ability to bring a greater degree of productively useful knowledge into the service of the capitalist. How does this knowledge relate to the concept of relations of production, and to the basic structural definition of class? As stated above, relations of production are relations of effective control over forces of production. Cohen correctly asserts that 'Labour power is a productive force, and one dimension of labour power is productively useful knowledge. It follows that scientific knowledge which is open to productive use is a productive force.'[67]

Notwithstanding Cohen's assertion, the possession of this scientific or technical knowledge is not the reason why such specialists are not members of the proletariat. It is the ownership of – that is, effective control over – this productive force (specialist knowledge) which enables the professional to command working conditions which are superior to those endured by non-owners of such productive knowledge or skills. The obvious difficulty which arises here is that many proletarians possess productively useful skills or knowledge and if such assets are to be taken as a *dimension of their labour power*, then why should the skill assets of the professional be treated any differently – as ownership of means of production? It's true that the level of skills possessed helps to explain why a surgeon enjoys better working conditions than a machinist, but working conditions (including subordination and domination in the production process) do not enter into a structural definition of class unless it can be shown that they derive directly from structural factors. Similarly, the different educational and occupational opportunities for gaining productively useful skills or knowledge available to different classes may tell us much about the mechanisms of (or absence of) class closure in particular societies, but neither educational provision nor levels of social mobility bear upon a structural *definition* of class locations in capitalism.

A better approach to this problem shifts the focus of attention away from the possession of skills, to the way in which such skills are often *used* in the workplace. To return to the top-salaried architect used in earlier examples: he uses his expert knowledge to make largely autonomous decisions about the deployment of capital assets which are owned by others. He has no legal ownership over the productive forces in question, but does exercise significant control over their use. The capitalist, as a non-expert, must entrust his capital assets to the technical skills of a whole range of experts and managers in order to maximise his return on those assets. As such, the managers and experts act as agents of the bourgeoisie. Those who exercise this type of effective control over productive forces which they do not own can be referred to as 'technocrats', whether their technical knowledge or skills are financial, managerial or practical. This group thus includes, but is not limited to, the controllers of 'assets in organization', identified by Erik Olin Wright.[68] These comments are not intended to apply to all employees whose job title includes the word manager, or to all those with technical qualifications or expertise. Many individuals in management positions, while enjoying a degree of responsibility, and often fulfilling a supervisory role over other workers, do not engage in the kind of autonomous decision making just described. Legal, commercial and technical constraints limit the autonomous control of most managers and skilled workers over the means of production which they use to such a minimal level that 'it ceases to make sense to talk about even residual forms of economic ownership'.[69]

Poulantzas argues that the agents who exercise the powers of resource allocation and who direct the labour process 'fulfil the "functions of capital" [and] occupy the place of capital, and thus belong to the bourgeois class even if they do not hold formal legal ownership. In all cases, therefore, the managers are an integral section of the bourgeois class.'[70] It is true that formal legal ownership is sometimes a poor guide to relations of effective control. Here, the attempt to locate managers (and other technocrats) in the bourgeoisie is rejected, not because they lack formal legal ownership over the productive forces with which they work, but because the control which they exercise over those assets is severely limited in a real sense. Technocrats cannot sell or bequeath the assets which they 'control', nor can they hire them out for personal gain. Generally, they are obliged to aim to meet the wider objectives of the legal owners of the assets although they do enjoy significant autonomy in deciding how such objectives may be met. Significantly, their control over productive forces is, by definition, not the type of control which enables them to avoid selling their labour power to the capitalist class.[71] By contrast the bourgeois enjoys greater control over his assets, nominating technocrats to act in his interests only in so far as it suits him to do so. The bourgeois can sell or bequeath his assets; or attempt to increase their value, by his own efforts or by placing his trust in technocrats. Crucially, the bourgeois can choose to live from the profit made by the work of others – he may choose to work, but need not do so in order to live.

The nature of the technocrats' control over the productive forces they use is significant for our analysis because it affects the likely attitude of the technocrat to potential changes in the economic structure. The control the technocrats enjoy is a product of their specialist knowledge, and the trappings associated with such expertise – in terms of status, working conditions and so on – are not threatened by certain forms of structural change, in the same way that the ownership privileges of the bourgeoisie may be threatened. The impact of nationalising essential industries, for example, would be very different for shareholders compared to senior, technically capable employees.

Having argued against the inclusion of the technocracy within the bourgeoisie, it is now necessary to defend their exclusion from the proletariat. The grounds for this exclusion are that technocrats exercise a degree of effective control over productive forces, aside from their own labour power. Now it was suggested earlier that this is sometimes true of proletarians, but that in the cases examined that this ownership was 'illusory'. The illusory nature of such ownership was asserted on the following grounds:

- The stated ownership does not free the workers from the need to sell their labour power.
- The ownership is 'adventitious'.

As for the first consideration, it has already been shown that technocrats *do* have to sell their labour power. (Although not because the means of production are of insufficient magnitude, but because the control which they exercise over those means of production is of the wrong *type*.) The second consideration is clearly where the difference between the two cases lies. In the case of the proletarians, the capitalist chooses between *a)* employing wage labourers to work on machines which belong to him, and *b)* employing wage labourers on condition that they own a machine. When he takes the second option, he does so because it places the burdens of ownership (maintenance, repair etc.) upon the workers. In the case of the technocrats, he cannot choose to continue to employ them (as technocrats) while retaining full control over the allocation and deployment of his means of production.

Technocrats, then, may be characterised by the following structural conditions: They own their own labour power which they sell to capitalists. They exercise control over means of production, but this control is limited in scope. (That is, they do not enjoy the full range of ownership rights over those means of production.) They do not legally 'own' the means of production, nor do they merely 'use' them. Rather, they make largely autonomous decisions about how and where those means of production should be used. To the extent that the technocrat's skills and knowledge are essential to the optimal allocation and deployment of means of production, the capitalist's control over those means of production is diminished. Occupations which are characteristically filled by technocrats may involve a lesser degree of subordination than typically proletarian ones. But a lack of subordination in the workplace is no more a part of the structural definition of class than is the relatively high salary which technocrats often attract.

It is important to recognise that the 'technocracy' is not equivalent to the petty-bourgeoisie, nor does it constitute a fraction of that class. Jon Elster argues that the petty-bourgeoisie 'comprises exploiters as well as exploited'[72] whereas John Roemer, while noting that 'the exploitation status of the petit-bourgeoisie is ambiguous', insists that they are a class who do not hire the labour power of others, and who do not sell their own labour power. (That is, they are neither exploiters, nor are they exploited.)[73] Donald Hodges has defined this class as those with sufficient capital to be self-employed, and even to employ one or two workers, but who still have to work themselves.[74] The advantage of Hodges' characterisation is that it views the petty-bourgeois as exactly what the term suggests; he is engaged in the commercial marketplace on his own behalf, but on a smaller scale than the bourgeois proper. This characterisation may also be framed in structural terms: The petty-bourgeoisie enjoy effective control over their own labour power. They own some means of production, but the nature and extent of those assets, and of their control over them, are such that they are not able to live without labouring but also that they do not have to sell their labour power to another.[75]

In this chapter we've looked at class consciousness and its relationship to behaviour, at how a structural definition of class location might be applied in various intermediate cases under capitalism and at how such definitions might reveal insights into the potential responses of members of those groups to certain structural changes. In the following chapter we'll consider these structural definitions of class in terms of the differences between capitalism and feudalism, which will also lead us on to comparing the modes of exploitation and modes of production in these two economic structures.

2.3 Economic Structures – Capitalism and Feudalism

As we noted in Section One, production relations are relationships of ownership or control of productive forces – they describe who owns what in the productive process. Marx used the term 'economic structure' to represent 'the totality of production relations' in a society.[76] Individuals who share similar production relations can be thought of as a class and the immediate producers – the workers – in capitalism and in feudalism are differentiated by their respective production relations.

Under capitalism most workers are proletarians – they are free wage labourers who own their own labour power and no other means of production. Under feudalism, most workers do not have full ownership rights over their own labour power (even after the demise of formal serfdom, extensive restrictions existed which limited the workers' ownership of their own labour power), but on the other hand, will often have some form of ownership or control over some means of production.

This short summary is somewhat idealised – as Cohen notes, 'real history exhibits important shadings and significant intermediate cases'.[77] This is particularly true in the case of societies based on serfdom, in which Vinogradoff observed 'a mixture of diverse classes of serfs and free men, which shaded off into each other by insensible degrees'.[78] The existence of such complications, though, does not preclude the possibility of identifying the essential features of feudal and capitalist societies.

Proletarians are immediate producers who 'own their labour power and no other productive force'.[79] As owners of their own labour power, proletarians are, in a significant sense, personally free. That is, they are free to sell their labour power to the highest bidder; they cannot be coerced into working for another. Yet, their lack of ownership of any other productive force; their lack of 'everything necessary for the realisation of [their] labour power'[80] provides the circumstances under which proletarians are compelled, on pain of starvation, to sell their labour power to some capitalist or other. This necessity means that the value of the reward received by the worker is generally the product of an inequitable negotiation, and therefore less than would otherwise have been the case. The difference between the value of the actual reward and the value which the worker could have negotiated without this necessity is what historical materialists call *surplus value*, or if measured in terms of the additional work performed to receive the same reward, *surplus labour*.

The freedom of the proletarian to sell his labour power as a commodity is not shared by slaves or serfs.[81] The slave-master and the manorial lord hold rights over the labour power of their 'subjects', whose subordination and exploitation are aspects of their personal unfreedom. The slave does not own his labour power as a commodity, but is himself a commodity, owned 'rump and stump' by another.[82]

Under feudalism (in England, at least) the personal unfreedom of the serf (or villein) was often compared, in legal doctrine, to that of the Roman slave.[83]Villeins were denied the right to hold property,[84] and were treated as the property of their masters, who could 'sell or otherwise alienate them if they like'.[85] Yet, in practice, villeins were taxed by the state independently of their lord,[86] and frequent cases of villeins buying their freedom with their own money are recorded.[87] The sale of villeins was extremely rare and Vinogradoff notes the importance of this point: 'the whole aspect of society and its work would have been different if the workman had been a saleable commodity passing easily from hand to hand. Nothing of this kind is to be noticed in the medieval system'.[88]

While the manorial lord did not in practice 'own' the persons of his villeins, he maintained significant control over their labour power. In the context of production relations, the freedom which the serf lacks, but which the proletarian enjoys, is the freedom to sell his labour power as a commodity, to the highest bidder. Although it was not uncommon for villeins to find work outside of their lord's manor, this always required a licence from the lord and, often, conditions were attached to the granting of the licence. Settlement outside of the manor was rarely permitted and was accompanied by the payment of a poll tax.

Thus, the serf's 'ownership rights' over his own labour power were severely limited. In the cultivation of his villein holding he could work as and when he pleased (providing that he was available to perform labour services when required), although he was not permitted to change the cultivation of his plot of his own accord. He was entitled to the fruits of this labour, excepting the payments of occasional dues, such as merchet and heriot. As labour services were commuted to rent in kind and later to money-rent, the villein gained more autonomy over his labour power, but the restrictions upon work outside the manor remained largely in place.

In contrast to the slave and the proletarian, the serf is conceived to be 'in possession of his own means of production, the necessary material labour conditions required for the realisation of his labour and the production of his means of subsistence'.[89] But although in 'possession' of such means of production, the serf does not hold full ownership rights over them. Typically, villein land cannot be sold, leased out or bequeathed by its cultivator and possessor, the serf.[90] According to legal doctrine the serf could be ousted from his plot at the will of the lord,[91] but in practice the majority enjoyed some security against dispossession: 'The state gave some protection to the villein, forbidding the lord to kill or maim him, or ruin him by depriving him of the essential means of production.'[92] Thus, although the villein's 'possession' of his means of subsistence was restricted, it was, to a certain extent, secure.

Feudal production relations, then, are characterised by forms of ownership in which the producers and their exploiters each hold different ownership rights over both the means of production and the labour power of serfs. The relationship between the serf's obligation to perform surplus labour and his 'possession' of his means of subsistence is discussed in the next section.

Modes of Exploitation

The mode of exploitation is 'the means whereby the producer is made to perform surplus labour'.[93] Under capitalism the mode of exploitation is (in ideal-typical terms at least) straightforward. The proletarian's lack of means of production forces him to sell his labour power in order to obtain his means of subsistence. The terms of the labour contract which arises from this sale are such as to ensure that the purchaser of labour power (the owner of the means of production, the capitalist) may extract surplus labour from the proletarian. Exploitation in this case is achieved by economic pressure (the economic necessity of the proletarian to avoid destitution or starvation) and is directly derived from the production relations which constitute the capitalist economic structure.

The feudal mode of exploitation is a more complicated matter. Marx comments that:

> The direct producer, according to our assumption, is to be found here in possession of his own means of production... He conducts his agricultural activity and the rural home industries connected with it independently...Under such conditions the surplus labour for the nominal owner of the land can only be extorted from them by other than economic pressure...Thus, conditions of personal dependence are requisite, a lack of personal freedom, no matter to what extent, and being tied to the soil as its accessory, bondage in the true sense of the word.[94]

Two contrasting interpretations of these passages have been suggested. Rodney Hilton, Eric Hobsbawm and others have argued that the serf, as an 'economically independent producer',[95] 'does not need to alienate his labour power in order to live'[96] and therefore 'the transfer of the surplus must be forced'.[97] Against this, Cohen asserts that the serf's 'possession' of his plot is not secure independently of his obligation to perform surplus labour.[98] The serf could be evicted from his holding following 'a default in paying rent or in the performance of services [or] any other transgression against the interests of the lord'.[99] Cohen suggests that the serf's obligation to perform surplus labour, the exploitation of his labour power, is achieved by the exercise of 'the authority of the superior over the producer's labour power'.[100] The serf's obligations are thus explained by his personal unfreedom. His enjoyments, on the other hand, are assured (to the extent that they are assured) by the protection afforded by the state, partly as representative of the interests of the monarchy in terms of revenue and stability, and partly in the collective interests of the lords. His enjoyments, then, are explained by the need to maintain the labour force: 'A certain degree of protection for the rights of the peasant was thus inevitable under the rule of feudal production. The peasant must...be assured of the means of economic reproduction if the most was to be got out of him.'[101]

It is the serf's 'conditions of personal dependence' upon the lord which enable the latter to exploit the former and (despite Marx's claim) these are not requisite because the serf is in possession of his plot. Indeed, the only security of possession enjoyed by the serf is that which the state imposes, which is designed to maintain the system of dependence. Exploitation under the feudal system, then, is extra-economic, but it is still derived from the feudal economic structure. Not, as in the capitalist case, from the virtual monopoly of the exploiting class over the means of production, but from their effective control over the persons and, more significantly, the labour power of the villeins.

As to non-villein labour, Kosminsky has demonstrated the importance of wage labour to Feudalism in England. He calculates that 'the obligatory labour of villeins probably covered less than half the requirements of the demesnes for labour power...numerous sections of the population were not supported by their own land and were dependent, in whole or in part, on wages'.[102] Of those whose income included wage payments, the largest single group were the villein cottars, who accounted for over half of the villein households on the small manors covered by Kosminsky's sources. While they engaged, to a greater or lesser extent, in wage labour, such employment bore very little resemblance to the *free* wage labour of the proletarian. Their labour power remained, to a significant extent, the property of the lord. Although in terms of proportions of income the cottar may sometimes appear more as a wage labourer than a villein, this wage labour involved a very strong element of 'coercive feudal exploitation'[103] derived from the cottar's incomplete ownership of his own labour power.

The free peasantry, who accounted for nearly 40 per cent of peasant households and cultivated nearly 30 per cent of the total agricultural land[104], were also, very often, drawn into manorial exploitation. Only 40 per cent held land sufficient to produce their means of subsistence and more than half of these, while personally free, held their land under villein tenure.[105] Free men holding 'in villeinage' were directly exploited in the same manner as true villeins but had come to this position, not by birth, but as a result of a 'contract'. In common with the proletarian, then, these men were forced, through their lack of means of production, to enter into an exploitative contract. In contrast to the proletarian, though, this contract was not merely a labour contract but one which usually involved significant elements of personal servility. Even free peasants who enjoyed free tenure were, virtually without exception, required to perform some labour services and to pay a variety of miscellaneous dues. Thus, despite the apparent challenge to the ideal-typical model of feudalism posed by the existence of a free peasantry, it is reasonable to endorse Kosminsky's assertion that peasant free tenure is comprehensible only in terms of its relationship to manorial villeinage and exploitation.[106] It remains true, though, that a society is 'less feudal' to the extent that it contains a genuine free peasantry.

Modes of Production

In most cases, the phrase 'mode of production' refers to the *purpose* of production.[107] The *purpose* of production under capitalism is to use exchange-value to produce more exchange-value and to endlessly repeat this process:

> ...it is only in so far as the appropriation of ever more and more wealth in the abstract becomes the sole motive of his operations, that he functions as a capitalist...Use-values must therefore never be looked upon as the real aim of the capitalist; neither must the profit on any single transaction. The restless never-ending process of profit-making alone is what he aims at.[108]

The capitalist mode of production is, then, in this sense, production for the sake of capital accumulation. It is distinguished from earlier modes of production, not because it aims to produce exchange-value (money) rather than use-value (goods), but because earlier production (which may have involved a significant degree of production for exchange-value) was not aimed at the accumulation of capital.

When Marx talks of pre-capitalist modes 'where not the exchange-value, but the use-value of the product predominates',[109] he is referring to production in which, even where productivity and commerce are sufficiently developed to allow a degree of production for exchange-value, the point of obtaining exchange-value is to convert it into use-value for the satisfaction of its owner's needs. (Including the payment of money-rent, which, when transferred to the feudal lord, is similarly used to furnish his needs, rather than to accumulate more exchange-value.)

Thus, when Sweezy identifies feudalism with 'a system of production for use',[110] it should be recognised that this system does not exclude the market or the production of goods for exchange-value. What it does exclude is the production of goods for the continual accumulation of exchange-value as an end in itself. In this vein F. Ya. Polyanski has argued that commodity production was functional to feudalism, an integral part of the system which was not external or antagonistic to it.[111]

The mode of production in pre-capitalist societies, then, may range from a system of production purely for use (i.e. products do not pass through a market between producer and consumer) to one with a developed system of commercial exchange and a money economy. It seems that pre-capitalist modes are most suitably defined by what they are not; that is, they are not geared towards production for the sake of accumulating capital.

Social Forms: Mode and Structure

The terms 'feudalism' and 'capitalism' are used by Marx to denote 'different economic epochs',[112] but what are the specific features which distinguish one epoch from another? Referring to the relationship between labourers and means of production, Marx comments that 'The specific manner in which this union is accomplished distinguishes the different economic epochs of the structure of society from one another.'[113] In the light of this text Cohen argues that 'From the Marxian viewpoint, social forms are distinguished and unified by their types of economic structure, as individuated by the production relations dominant within them.'[114] Elsewhere, though, Marx implies a modal definition of capitalism: 'Capitalism is abolished root and branch by the bare assumption that it is personal consumption and not enrichment that works as the compelling motive...The capitalist...must accumulate capital.'[115] This passage suggests that a capitalist social form may be defined as one in which production is oriented at the accumulation of capital. Cohen notes that, as a matter of historical fact,[116] 'societies falling under the structural definition also satisfy the modal definition, and vice-versa' but suggests that 'the factual correlation may be relatively accidental. We need to show that it is more or less necessary, something to be expected.'[117] In terms of the individuation of social forms, then, Cohen subordinates 'modal' properties to 'structural' properties; the mode of production can only be asserted as a defining feature of a social form if there exist historical *and* theoretical correlations between mode and structure. Nevertheless, it must be accepted that Marx saw both the capitalist economic structure and the capitalist mode of production as necessary conditions for the characterisation of a social form as 'capitalist'.

The defining characteristic of feudalism has been the subject of some debate among historians. Paul Sweezy identifies the 'crucial feature' of feudalism as the prevalence of a 'system of production for use'[118] and this view is endorsed by Hobsbawm.[119] Maurice Dobb explicitly rejects this approach, arguing that feudalism should be defined by the fact that 'the producer is in possession of his means of production as an individual producing unit'.[120] Clearly, Sweezy has identified an aspect of the feudal mode of production, and Dobb's comments relate to the feudal economic structure. From a Marxian perspective, feudal society involves both of these elements, but the defining characteristic of a social form is structural, rather than modal not least because structural properties can be linked to the range of behavioural options available to the producing class in a way that modal properties cannot.

2.4 Historical Materialism and Historical Change

In Section One we looked briefly at Cohen's 'development thesis' and 'primacy thesis'. Here we can take a more detailed look at each of these and consider some criticisms of them. We'll also look at the concept of *functional explanation*[121] upon which the use of these theses in historical materialism depends.

The Development Thesis

If the superstructure is to be explained by the economic structure and the latter in turn by the level of development of the productive forces, then it is necessary to ask how this development is itself to be explained. Cohen bases his explanation of productive force development upon beliefs about human nature and the human condition. Arguing that humans are sufficiently intelligent to be able to improve their material situation and sufficiently rational to be disposed to do so, given their historical situation of scarcity, he asserts that 'the productive forces tend to develop throughout history'.[122] This *tendential* statement 'requires that it is in the nature of the forces to develop' but 'does not entail that the forces always develop, nor even that they never decline'.[123] Thus the 'development thesis' is not embarrassed by certain exceptions to the stated tendency and should not be expected to explain examples of 'abnormal' processes or occurrences. A criticism of this approach which is anticipated by Cohen is that human rationality is not a trans-historical constant but a context-dependent variable. His response is that there are *certain* permanent attributes of human nature which provide sufficient motivation to develop the productive forces. This is not an unreasonable claim given that the need to produce the means of subsistence, reproduction and security provides the required motivation and derives from a universal instinct for survival.

S.H. Rigby offers two general criticisms of the development thesis. Although these arguments do not inflict serious damage on the development thesis, they do raise interesting questions about the development of the productive forces. Firstly, he suggests that both 'need' and 'scarcity' are relative concepts which vary according to historical circumstances.[124] He envisages a 'primitive society' in which needs are minimal and means, in relation, are plentiful. It is difficult to conceive such a state of peace and plenty surviving for any significant length of time. Abundance typically promotes internal population growth and attracts migrants from less plentiful situations and this process alone may ensure that a situation of scarcity would soon be restored. Furthermore, Rigby's (correct) assertion that need is a relative concept suggests that as the necessities of life are catered for, new needs arise. In addition to compelling wants such as status and authority (which may indeed vary considerably according to circumstance) the need for individual and group security stimulates significant desire to continually increase the efficiency of the production of use-values. When human rationality is seen as 'situated' in a context of competition within and between interactive societies, then the need for security is manifested in the need for development. Societies which do not develop technologically will be at a significant disadvantage to those which do.

Of course, in any historical situation, there are competing needs which may inhibit development of the productive forces. The need for a sense of identity usually involves some notion of continuity, and this is reflected in the reverence for tradition and custom in many societies. But a sense of identity, like other human 'needs', is dependent upon survival, and therefore on the development of the productive forces. In short, the fact that both need and scarcity are relative concepts does not mean that situations in which neither is present in sufficient measure to influence behaviour are any more than isolated and temporary exceptions to the general historical situation of scarcity which confronts humankind.

Rigby's second criticism concerns the gulf between the rate of productive development under capitalism and that found in earlier societies. He argues that while pre-capitalist economic structures fail to 'systematically develop productivity', development under capitalism is so rapid that it cannot be explained as 'merely a speeded-up version of some trans-historical tendency'.[125] The claim that pre-capitalist relations of production do not systematically develop the forces is unquestionably consistent with Marx. In fact the point is emphasised – only under capitalist relations of production does the incentive to develop the forces 'arise from the nature of the production [system] itself'.[126] Pre-capitalist relations do not systematically promote development but, rather, *enable* development which is stimulated by the rationality and intelligence of humans, discussed above. Rigby also makes the more controversial claim that some economic structures possess an 'inbuilt tendency towards stagnation or even crisis and regression'.[127] The cases that Rigby cites though are not exceptions to the development of the forces under pre-capitalist structures but a set of historical situations which represent an important aspect of historical materialism: that 'at a certain stage of their development, the material productive forces of society come in conflict with the existing relations of production...within which they have been at work hitherto'.[128] These structures inhibit development, not because of an inbuilt tendency to do so but because eventually every structure will develop the forces to a stage where it is no longer able to promote further development.

Having discounted the possibilities of fossilisation, regression and miscarriage as 'forbidden' by Marx in the 1859 *Preface*, he notes that *temporary* fossilisation and regression are possible as part of the era of social revolution, which may last for centuries.[129] The relegation of such periods of stagnation or decline to a qualification of the main theses is curious. By doing this, Cohen leaves himself open to the charge that these phases merely fall into the category of random exceptions to the tendency identified in the development thesis; that they are no more than 'abnormalities' which a theory of history should not be expected to explain. It has been noted above, though, that Marx's theory of history does offer an explanation of these periodic interruptions to the development of the productive forces. Given that such phases may last for significant time periods it seems reasonable to award them a more prominent place in the theory of history.

The development thesis, as stated by Cohen, is based upon judgements about human rationality and intelligence 'in the context of the inclemency of nature'.[130] It is suggested that certain aspects of these factors are sufficiently trans-historical to warrant the assertion that a tendency may be detected among what may otherwise appear as a 'miscellany of uncoordinated reasons'.[131] It is also valid to identify as a tendency the way in which the productive forces periodically stagnate as they come into conflict with the relations of production. The development thesis may thus be usefully recast as follows: The productive forces tend to develop throughout history *through alternating phases of growth and stagnation*.

It could, of course, be argued that the tendency of the forces to develop arises out of basic and virtually universal features of the human condition (rationality, intelligence and the historical situation of scarcity) whereas the tendency to alternate in the stated fashion occurs only in the context of social relations of production. From this assertion it might be concluded that the latter tendency exists not *in the nature of* the productive forces but in the nature of the relationship between the forces and a succession of economic structures. However, this tendency is not asserted in connection with any particular series of economic structures but in connection with the fact that economic structures do exist and do have a relationship with the development of the forces. The existence of economic structures is as much a part of the human condition as the inclemency of nature and thus the tendency of the forces to periodically stagnate or regress is as much a feature of the *nature* of the forces as the overall tendency towards development. From this revised perspective the examples given by Rigby may be explained not as abnormalities beyond the scope of the theory, but as illustrations of the tendency of the productive forces to periodically stagnate or regress. Of course, some exceptions to the theory may still remain but at least historians may be clearer about what they are exceptions to. This is important because it helps us to view the transition from one structure to the next as a process, not a moment, which in turn allows us to understand both the Soviet experience and many of the developments we're witnessing in contemporary Western society.

The class struggle and the era of social revolution are given further consideration in the discussions on the 'primacy thesis' and on functional explanation, below.

The Primacy Thesis

The primacy thesis, as stated by Cohen, asserts that 'the nature of a set of production relations is explained by the level of development of the productive forces embraced by it (to a far greater extent than vice-versa)'.[132] Cohen notes that while a given level of development rules out certain economic structures, this does not in itself establish the primacy of the productive forces, as the constraint is symmetrical. If, however, this 'mutual constraint' is combined with the implication of the development thesis – that the growth of the forces cannot be subverted indefinitely – then economic structures must 'rise and fall according as they enable or impede that growth'.[133] Primacy is thus attributed to the forces as 'contradictions' must be resolved in favour of continued development at the expense of the economic structure.

The explanatory primacy of the forces is qualified, though, by the influence exerted by the production relations over the rate of development and the particular path which that development takes. That the relations promote development is entailed by the primacy thesis: They obtain *because* of this property. Stated in these terms, the primacy of the productive forces derives from the proposition that a given economic structure obtains when *and because* it fulfils the function of developing the forces. That is: 'the character of the forces *functionally* explains the character of the relations'.[134] Accordingly, stable relations of production are so because they are compatible with development of the forces. When the forces develop to the level at which the existing structure no longer promotes their advance, the relations are revolutionised: 'the old relations cease to exist because they no longer favour the forces and the new relations come into being because they are apt to do so'.[135] Cohen notes the likelihood of a time lag as the economic structure undergoes this transition. During this period the relations of production of the old order persist for a while after they have become dysfunctional for the development of the forces. Here, 'the character of the relations is explained by their suitability to a *past* stage in the development of the forces'.[136] Cohen acknowledges that the case for the primacy of the forces which he submits is not conclusive. He suggests that the most promising alternative may be to propose a development thesis for production relations, but argues that it 'would be extremely difficult to substantiate any such claim'.[137] Rigby, though, does accord primacy to the relations: 'the most profitable reading of Marx is one which stresses the primacy of a society's relations of production'.[138] Against the primacy of the forces, Rigby asserts that historical evidence shows that economic structures *do not* correspond to specific levels of development of the forces.

Firstly, he argues that the same level of development can support various economic structures; that the category of pre-capitalist class society 'takes up rather a large slice of human history' and includes 'a variety of forms of class relations'.[139] However, these various forms of class relations share significant, definitional features. They involve exploitation of non-free immediate producers via non-contractual relations for the production of use-values, or exchange values (but not for the accumulation of capital). If these features obtain throughout a large slice of human history then it is not surprising that the category which they define also does so. Similarly, the 'level' of development to which these structures correspond is a *range* within which much of human history falls; that where some surplus is produced, but not enough to allow capitalist production; production for the accumulation of capital. Rigby suggests that little is gained by claiming that such a variety of economic structures 'correspond to a level of development which yields some surplus but less than capitalism'.[140] But the primacy thesis makes a greater claim than this. The claim is that these structures shared common features, that these features were present *because* surplus was limited and that they were replaced by capitalist structures *when and because* surplus reached the required level (the level at which production for the accumulation of capital became possible).

Rigby's second argument against the primacy thesis is that different levels of development of the productive forces may result in the same set of class relations. He cites the 'classic example' of this as Marx's division of the capitalist era into two periods, manufacture and large-scale industry. Again, though, while the forces of production have developed massively under capitalism, the level of development has remained within a specific range: sufficient surplus is produced to allow for production for accumulation of capital, but not enough to 'make it no longer true that most of life and time and energy must be spent joylessly producing means to imperative ends'.[141]

The Transitional Phase

The transition from feudalism to capitalism is the subject of Rigby's third objection to the primacy thesis: 'The problem is that Marx's whole analysis of the transition to capitalism is based on the assumption that capitalist relations of production were introduced prior to...the new types of technology which allowed social productivity and the level of surplus to be increased.'[142] It is indeed true that the advent of capitalist relations was followed by massive growth of the productive forces; it is in the nature of capitalism to promote such growth. However, capitalist relations could not have arisen if the forces had not already been developed to the level where production for the accumulation of capital was possible. This development necessarily took place under pre-capitalist structures, *before* the advent of capitalist relations. Even if Rigby doubts that the productive forces *tend* to develop throughout history, it cannot be denied that (on the whole) they *have* developed (otherwise capitalism could not have arisen). Thus the advent of capitalist relations of production was necessarily prior to *and* preceded by further growth of the productive forces. In other words, the emergence of capitalism was preceded by development under the relative stability of feudalism and was prior to the stable growth promoted by the capitalist structure.

The emergence of a new set of relations (as noted above) is not viewed as an event, but as a process or, more accurately, a series of processes. The 1859 *Preface* asserts that:

1. 'At a certain stage of their development, the material productive forces of society come into conflict with the existing relations of production...within the framework of which they have hitherto operated'
2. 'From forms of development of the productive forces these relations turn into their fetters'
3. 'At that point an era of social revolution begins'
4. This brings about a 'change in the economic structure'[143]

Now, the primacy of the productive forces during the period encompassed by these processes is maintained by Cohen via the proposition that when the relations are dysfunctional for the development of the forces, they obtain because they *were* functional up to a recently surpassed level of development. But the relations do not pass from this dysfunctional situation directly and immediately into the new, functional economic structure. Cohen's formulation holds true for the prelude to the era of social revolution, (stages 1 and 2, above) but not for the revolutionary era itself (stages 3 and 4, above).

The transition from feudalism to capitalism in England may serve as a suitable illustration of this point. Marx notes that by the end of the fourteenth century, 'feudalism had practically disappeared' and the 'immense majority of the population consisted then, and to a still larger extent, in the fifteenth century, of free peasant proprietors'.[144] These free peasant proprietors were not serfs, but nor were they proletarians, for, as Cohen notes, 'a surplus was...extracted by non-contractual means'.[145] Thus, from this point until the proliferation of capitalist relations, based upon free wage-labour the economic structure was characterised by post-serf, pre-proletarian producers. (This is not a phenomenon unique to England: 'Whenever it [capitalism] appears, the abolition of serfdom has been long effected.'[146] See also the discussion on pre-revolutionary Russia in Chapter 3.1.)

The character of the economic structure during the era of social revolution is, then, of a specifically transitional type. In this case the transitional form occurs because of the time lag between the availability of forces which, for their development, require capitalist relations, and the actual establishment of such relations. The level of development of the forces explains the character of the structure, during this period, only in so far as the changes in the relations represent moves towards meeting the 'needs' for the further development of the forces. It was noted earlier that the primacy of the forces is qualified by the influence exerted by the economic structure over the rate of development and the particular path which that development takes. These influences are greatly increased during the entire period of transition and particularly during the era of social revolution. The nature of the forces during this era is, then, to a significant extent explained by the transitional character of the economic structure; development intermittently stalls and falters amid local (sectional) and sporadic bursts of growth as the relations adjust to meet the requirements of the existing and potential forces of production.

The overall primacy of the forces remains intact and can be seen at work in the way that the social revolution is resolved. The need for the further development of the forces explains the character of the structure which emerges from the era of social revolution and achieves stability because of its ability to develop the forces at the then existing level. *During* the social revolution, however, it is the character of the economic structure which explains the character of the forces. And this is a significant claim. Not only because the periods of history to which it relates are long and important generally, but also because they are necessary and recurring stages in the development of the productive forces. This claim is also important today, as we enter the transitional phase out of capitalism.

Functional Explanation

Functional explanation, of which the primacy thesis is an example, is, for Cohen a necessary part of Marx's theory of history: 'I do not see how historical materialism can avoid it, for better or for worse.'[147] As will be seen, though, it is a contested procedure and here some of the most common objections to its use in the social sciences will be discussed.

First of all it is useful to examine just what is meant by the term 'functional explanation' in this context. Suppose there is an event *e* and its consequence *f*. To say that *e* is functionally explained by *f* is not to say that *f* caused *e*, for that would be to argue that an event was caused by its consequence. The form of the explanation is that *e* occurred because the situation was such that an event of type *E* would cause an event of type *F*. Cohen provides an example from the biological sciences:

'Birds developed hollow bones because hollow bones facilitate flight is an explanation of the functional type with *E* being possession of hollow bones by birds and *F* being the facilitation of flight which is a consequence of *E*.'[148]

And one from the social sciences:

'Scale of production is large in a certain industry because large-scale reduces costs in that kind of industry.'[149] In this case, *E* is large-scale production and *F* is reduced costs, which is a consequence of *E*.

It is important to note that because an event of type E would cause an event of type F, it does not necessarily follow that e occurred *because* it would cause an event of type F: 'A may be functional for B even when it is false that A exists, or has the character that it does, *because* its existence or character is functional for B.'[150] In order to show that A occurs *because* it is functional for B, evidence is required beyond that which shows that A *is* functional for B. Jon Elster asserts that a functional explanation is only valid if it is supported by a plausible account of *how* B functionally explains A. Cohen suggests that even if the mechanism is unknown, the claim that B functionally explains A can be validated if evidence exists 'across an appropriately varied range of instances' that 'whenever A would be functional for B, A appears'.[151]

To return to the examples given earlier – the case of the birds and their hollow bones is accepted by both Cohen and Elster as a genuine functional explanation. The mechanism of natural selection provides the elaboration of *how* the functional fact explains why birds have hollow bones. But Cohen goes further than this. He argues that before Darwin identified the mechanism, natural historians were justified in their belief that the functionality of certain features in certain species explained the presence of those features. The point which Cohen makes here is that 'it is sometimes rational to have confidence in a functional explanation in advance of having a good idea of what the mechanism may be'.[152] Thus when Elster argues that 'Functional analysis...has no place in the social sciences, because there is no sociological analogy to the theory of natural selection'[153] it could be argued that because the 'sociological analogy' has not yet been identified, that does not necessarily mean that it does not exist. It may also be argued that even if a general mechanism which covers all types of sociological phenomena does *not* exist, functional-explanatory claims in *particular cases* may still be valid in the social sciences. And this argument will be strengthened if, in some such cases, the elaboration (of how the functionality of a given phenomenon explains its existence or character) can be specified. If a sufficiently large and varied set of cases can be satisfactorily explained and elaborated, then it may be possible to identify common features of these cases and then to formulate a general theory, but the validity of functional explanation in the social sciences does not rest upon the success of such a project. What seems a more realistic proposition is the formulation, not of a single sociological analogy to natural selection but of a series of analogies which refer to distinct categories of sociological phenomena.

The second of the examples given above – that of large-scale production in a specified industry – may serve as a suitable starting point for developing such analogies. How does the fact that large-scale production reduces costs explain the diffusion of this particular practice across an industry? Cohen suggests that 'sometimes it will be because the functional fact selects in favour of firms which for accidental reasons expand their scale, sometimes that wise planners recognise the functional fact and act accordingly, and sometimes both elements will figure'.[154] But this provides only half of the required elaboration. In order to uncover the mechanism in full it's necessary to establish not only how large-scale production is adopted, but also how the functional fact selects. In this case the answer is that under the competitive market, survival prospects are increased by the adoption of profit-maximising strategies.[155] Cohen notes that the *purposive* elaboration may apply even when the industrial units do not operate in a competitive market, 'the decision makers may be Gosplanners, setting the course of an industry wholly subject to their will'.[156] But if the units do not exist in a competitive environment, then why should reduced costs be desirable? This is not to say that they are not desirable, merely to suggest that without knowledge of why they are desirable the elaboration is incomplete.

If the industrial units do exist in a competitive environment, then the desirability of reduced costs is explained by the profit-maximising aspect of cost reduction and the survival-promoting aspect of profit-maximising strategies. If, then, the analysis is restricted to firms operating in a competitive economy then the functional explanation may be restated: Scale of production is large in a certain industry because large-scale facilitates survival in the competitive market. It has been shown that large-scale may come into being for either rational or accidental reasons, but why should it persist at the expense of small-scale production? The answer is entailed by the functional fact that large-scale facilitates survival in the competitive market.

Is it possible, then, to generalise that in competitive situations functional facts which refer to survival-promoting functions will normally yield valid functional-explanatory claims? The problem here is that while the functional fact entails the (chronologically) second part of the elaboration (why the functional phenomena persists), it says nothing about the (chronologically) first part of the elaboration (how the phenomena arose in the first place). But, as has been stated above, the means by which the functional behaviour arises is not central to the task of confirming the validity of a functional-explanatory claim. In order to determine whether large-scale exists in a given industry *because* it is functional, it is not necessary to know why large-scale was adopted, but why it survived. This is because the practice may be functional, and may persist *because* it is functional, even if it did not arise because it was functional, but for accidental reasons.

It can be argued then that the exact nature of the *immediate* cause of the phenomenon to be explained is not of crucial importance to the elaboration. In the terminology of the industrial example: So long as scale of production is not uniform throughout the industry, so long as variation exists, then those firms whose scale is survival-promoting will persist at the expense of those whose scale is detrimental. The generalisation given above can, then, be restated: *In competitive situations, functional facts which refer to survival-promoting functions will normally yield valid functional-explanatory claims when the functional strategy (or event or process) was one of a set whose members were variably suited to promoting survival.*[157] Thus this part of the elaboration is not too distantly related to Darwin's notion of chance variation. Nor is the survival-promoting nature of the functions in question (the functions to which the generalisation is limited) unlike Spencer's notion of survival of the fittest.

The application of this generalisation may be illustrated with reference to the proposition that the character of an economic structure is functionally explained by the level of development of the productive forces which it embraces. The first important point is that the exact nature of the immediate cause of the initial emergence of, for example, capitalist relations is not crucial to the elaboration of how such relations came to dominate the economic structure. It may be historically interesting, but it is not central to the explanation.[158] It is likely that other, less suitable relations were also employed, but what is important *in the present enquiry* is why capitalist relations persisted while others did not.[159] In order to show that the given relations persisted *because* of their functionality for the development of the productive forces it would, then, 'only' be necessary to demonstrate that:

1. During the era of social revolution
a. Various relations of production are available and are variously functional for the development of the forces.
b. These relations exist in a competitive environment (within and/or between societies).
c. Relations which develop the forces have a survival advantage over those which do not (or which do so less efficiently).
2. Those relations which possess the stated advantage survive the revolutionary era and come to dominate the structure in

the post-revolutionary period of stable development.

It may be the case that the competition and the survival advantage (in 1*b* and 1*c* respectively) operate through those persons who hold the 'effective control' in the relevant relations of production. But these components of the argument are properties which relate to the relations themselves. This is important because too often social revolution is seen as necessarily involving violent conflict between individuals or groups, whereas the only *necessary* conflict in revolutionary periods is that between relations of production, in which one set of relations are displaced by another. It is possible that a transformation from one economic structure to another may take place entirely by 'adaptive metamorphosis'.

In this section the form of functional explanations and their use in the social sciences have been examined and provisionally endorsed. The absence of a general theory of elaboration is not accepted as a sufficient reason for rejecting this type of explanation, nor is the argument that particular cases of functional explanation are only acceptable if the relevant elaboration has been specified. Cohen's view that functional explanations may be valid in advance of the knowledge of how they are to be elaborated has been accepted. But it remains true that such elaborations would greatly increase the case for endorsing any particular functional-explanatory claim. With this in mind, an attempt has been made to construct a generalised elaboration which may be valid for a particular specified set of cases of functional explanation. It is not suggested that functional explanations are only valid if they meet the criteria specified here. Nor, of course, would the falsehood of this generalisation invalidate the use of functional explanation in the social sciences.

2.5 Bourgeois Revolutions in Historical Materialism

What are the processes which historical materialism might

require or expect to occur during the transition from feudalism to capitalism? What, that is, are the essential or characteristic features of the bourgeois revolution? This chapter will consider the processes which are theoretically required by the differences between the two social forms in question – feudalism and capitalism – and also, any further processes which were considered by Marx to be essential, likely or possible features of the bourgeois revolution. The key features of each of the two relevant social forms are summarised below:

Economic Structure

Under capitalism the means of production are concentrated in the hands of non-producers. Producers own no relevantly significant means of production, but hold full ownership rights over their own labour power. Under feudalism, producers and non-producers each hold different rights over both the labour power of the producers and some of the means of production.

Mode of Production

Under capitalism, the purpose of production is the accumulation of capital. Under feudalism the purpose of production is the creation of use-value, or the accumulation of exchange-value, for the purpose of acquiring more use-value.

The mode of exploitation under feudalism is non-economic – producers are obliged to perform surplus labour by virtue of their personal subordination; their incomplete ownership of their own labour power. Under capitalism, producers, as owners of their own labour power, are under no such obligation. It is their lack of relevant ownership rights over means of production which obliges them to sell their labour power on terms which ensure their exploitation. The capitalist mode of exploitation is economic.

Form of Surplus Labour

Under feudalism surplus labour takes the form of rent – including labour rent, rent in kind and money-rent, but always feudal rent based on dues which arise from a form of personal subordination, and distinct from capitalist ground rent in which means of production are let according to free contract. Under capitalism, surplus labour is extracted as profit including capitalist ground rent as well as 'working' profit on industrial, mercantile and finance capital.

* * *

Under both feudalism and capitalism the mode of exploitation and the form of surplus labour are conceptually linked to – and derived from – the dominant production relations. The era of social revolution – the replacement of one economic structure with another – will, then, also include corresponding upheavals in the mode of exploitation and in the form of surplus labour. The purpose of production is also related to the economic structure. Under capitalism the purpose of production is the accumulation of capital but the creation of capital requires particular economic structural conditions:

> In themselves money and commodities are no more capital than are the means of production and of subsistence. They want transforming into capital. But this transformation itself can only take place under certain conditions that centre in this, viz., that two very different kinds of commodity possessors must come face to face and into contact; on the one hand, the owners of money, means of production, means of subsistence, who are eager to increase the sum of values they possess by buying other people's labour-power; on the other hand, free labourers, the sellers of their own labour-power, and therefore the sellers of labour.[160]

The existence of these different kinds of commodity possessors – the bourgeoisie and the proletariat – is an essential precondition for the advent of the capitalist system. Their creation is:

> the process which clears the way for the capitalist system...the process which takes away from the labourer the possession of his means of production [and] transforms, on the one hand, the social means of subsistence and of production into capital, on the other hand, the immediate producers into wage labourers.[161]

The creation of capital, 'the transformation of the individualised and scattered means of production into socially concentrated ones, of the pygmy property of the many into the huge property of the few' accompanies the 'expropriation of the great mass of the people from the soil, from the means of subsistence, and from the means of labour' and forms the 'prelude to the history of capital'.[162] Marx repeatedly emphasises the importance of the creation of a proletariat in the process of bourgeois revolution: 'the capitalist mode of production and of accumulation, and therefore capitalist private property, have for their fundamental condition the annihilation of self-earned private property; in other words, the expropriation of the labourer'.[163]

This expropriation creates a class of 'free labourers, in the double sense that neither they themselves form part and parcel of the means of production, as in the case of slaves, bondsmen, &c., nor do the means of production belong to them, as in the case of peasant proprietors; they are therefore, free from, unencumbered by, any means of production of their own'.[164] With these changes in the economic structure and the mode of production come changes in the mode of exploitation as 'the dull compulsion of economic relations completes the subjection of the labourer to the capitalist'.[165] The capitalist system 'pre-supposes the complete separation of the labourers from all property in the means by which they can realise their labour'.[166]

In line with the central theses of historical materialism, it is the economic structural changes which assume the dominant role in the process of bourgeois revolution. As has been shown above, these structural changes create the conditions for the modal elements of capitalist production – the purpose of production, the mode of exploitation and the form of surplus labour. These revolutionary developments in the economic structure and the mode of production are conceptually required by the nature of the bourgeois revolution. In addition to these processes, Marx also identifies various supplementary features of the transition from feudalism to capitalism.

Owing to the relationship between the level of development of the productive forces and the emergence of capitalism, historical materialism sees the bourgeois revolution as developing in conjunction with processes of industrialisation and urbanisation: 'Modern industry alone, and finally, supplies, in machinery, the lasting basis of capitalistic agriculture, expropriates radically the enormous majority of the agricultural population, and completes the separation between agriculture and rural domestic industry, whose roots – spinning and weaving – it tears up'.[167] Industrialisation and urbanisation result not just in a change in the pace of life but also, in combination with the development of the capitalist system, a dramatic change in the pace of change. As the capitalist system begins to establish itself a 'boundless thirst for surplus labour arises from the nature of production itself'.[168] This boundless thirst for surplus labour provides a stimulus for the massive and unprecedented growth in productive capacity which is characteristic of capitalist production and which begins during the era of bourgeois revolution.

Rapid industrialisation and urbanisation bring with them a degree of misery and add to the 'fearful and painful'[169] experience of the revolution in the economic structure. In describing the emergence of capitalism in England, Marx notes the plight of the agricultural population and refers to the 'usurpation of feudal and clan property under circumstances of reckless terrorism'.[170] Marx also asserts the way in which 'brute force' – which plays no central role in the capitalist mode of exploitation – is a necessary component of the bourgeois revolution; and in this connection he also asserts the essential role of the state in this period:

Under capitalist production:

> Direct force, outside economic conditions, is of course still used, but only exceptionally. In the ordinary run of things, the labourer can be left to the 'natural laws of production', i.e., to his dependence on capital, a dependence springing from, and guaranteed in perpetuity by, the conditions of production themselves[171]

...and yet

> It is otherwise during the historic genesis of capitalist production. The bourgeoisie, at its rise, wants and uses the power of the state to 'regulate' wages, i.e. to force them within the limits suitable for surplus value making, to lengthen the working day and to keep the labourer himself in the normal degree of dependence. This is an essential element of the so-called primitive accumulation.[172]

Marx further suggests that the emerging bourgeoisie employs the power of the state, 'the concentrated and organised force of society, to hasten, hot-house fashion, the process of transformation of the feudal mode of production into the capitalist mode, and to hasten the transition'.[173]

Jon Elster suggests that 'Marx perceived the classical bourgeois revolutions as the transition from absolute to constitutional monarchy with a republican interregnum'[174] and cites Marx's comments that 'everywhere the transition from absolute to constitutional monarchy is effected only after fierce struggles and after passage through a republican form'.[175] From this, Elster concludes that 'it would be wrong to focus on the transition from monarchy to republic as *the* revolution; this is only a stage in a process whose overall form is "two steps forward, one step backward"'.[176] Elster is certainly correct in saying that Marx did not view the establishment of a republic as *the* bourgeois revolution. But any reading of Marx's comments on the displacement of feudalism by capitalism clearly shows that even the transition from absolute to constitutional monarchy represented, for Marx, merely one stage of the social revolutionary era. Furthermore, as essentially *political* events, these 'classical bourgeois revolutions' – while carrying some symbolic significance as revolutionary 'moments' – largely *reflect* the broader and more important economic and social developments.[177]

Elster also notes another feature which, according to Marx, accompanies the republican stage of the 'classical' bourgeois revolutions: the emergence of an embryonic proletarian movement. But the potential of this early proletarian action must not be overestimated, given the broader historical context:

> If...the proletariat overthrows the political rule of the bourgeoisie, its victory will only be temporary, only an element in the service of the bourgeois revolution itself... as long as in the course of its history, in its 'movement', the material conditions have not yet been created which make necessary the abolition of the bourgeois mode of production and therefore also the definitive overthrow of the political rule of the bourgeoisie.[178]

And here Marx also warns that the bourgeois revolution can only succeed if the 'economic conditions' for the rule of the bourgeois class have become ripe: 'Men build a new world for themselves...

from the historical achievements of their declining world. In the course of their development they first have to *produce* the *material conditions* of a new society itself, and no exertion of mind or will can free them from this fate.'[179]

In addition to this material pre-requisite, the key features of the bourgeois revolution are summarised below:

1. Fundamental to the bourgeois revolution is the transition from a feudal economic structure to a capitalist one. Essentially, the bourgeois revolution consists in this process. Central to this transition are:

a. The expropriation of the immediate producers.

b. The dissolution of feudal obligations.

c. The concentration of the means of production.

2. Following from these economic structural changes (conceptually and/or temporally) are changes in the modal properties of production.

a. The purpose of production becomes the accumulation of capital.

b. The mode of exploitation becomes almost solely economic.

c. The form of surplus labour changes from rent to profit.

3. The bourgeois revolution develops over a period which includes a time of rapid industrialisation and urbanisation.

4. Violence and 'brute force' are likely features of the transitional period.

5. The state plays an essential role in governing the conditions of production during the bourgeois revolution and is used to hasten the transition.

6. The transition from absolute to constitutional monarchy and the short-lived advent of a republic are neither conceptually necessary, nor are they deemed essential components of the process by Marx. Their occurrence in the 'classical' bourgeois revolutions, though, is noted.

7. Of a similar conceptual status is the emergence of an

embryonic proletarian movement. Any success for such a movement could only be temporary, consisting largely of a seizure of political power. Any such proletarian victory would (eventually) be doomed to failure owing to the absence of the material conditions necessary for the establishment of socialism. Attempts by a proletarian regime to use political power to impose production relations for which the prevailing material conditions were unsuitable, would be the attempts of the political tail to wag the economic dog and could not – according to historical materialism – achieve lasting success. Marx noted that in France 'the bloody action of the people' could 'only serve to spirit away...The ruins of feudalism' and to 'prepare the way for [the bourgeoisie]'.[180]

* * *

The close correlation between Marx's conception of the bourgeois revolution and the course of Russian history since the middle of the nineteenth-century is evident from the study of that historical period we now address in Section Three.

3. Russia and the Soviet Union

It may seem strange that in the following pages questions such as the size of peasant allotments in late nineteenth-century Russia are given considerably more attention than the entire course and development of, for example, the two world wars combined. This is not because those events were not important, but because they are not particularly relevant to the present inquiry and have been extensively covered elsewhere. The world is not short of general histories of Russia and the Soviet Union, and there's little point in writing another. The aim here, rather, is to gather together and present the facts relevant to the case made in Section 1 – that the course of Russian and Soviet history, from emancipation to the collapse of the Soviet Union, represents a bourgeois revolution, in line with Marx's development of that concept.

3.1 Pre-Revolutionary Russia
The Emancipation of the Serfs

The first article of the emancipation regulations of 1861 announced that 'The enserfment of peasants settled on landlord's estates and of domestic servants is abolished forever' and that these former serfs 'are granted by right the status of free rural inhabitants, personally and with respect to property'.[181] Yet the now 'free' Russian peasants still lacked full ownership rights over their persons (and therefore their labour power) and also over the means of subsistence and production upon which their survival depended. As Sergei Pushkarev has noted, beyond the general statements guaranteeing peasant freedom, the reform regulations contained 'a multitude of qualifications and complexities'.[182]

In its public proclamations the Tsarist regime declared its concern to safeguard the wellbeing of the peasantry, as well as that of the landowners: 'The peasant should immediately feel that his lot has been improved; the landowner should at once be satisfied that his interests are protected, and stable political order should not be disturbed for one moment in any locality.'[183] This concern for the lot of the peasantry, though, did not extend to the inclusion of any of their representatives on any of the commissions or other bodies which considered the terms of the emancipation. The commissions consisted exclusively of the representatives of the state and the landowning nobility.

For their part, the landowners, or at least a section of them, expressed their concern for the moral fibre of the peasants in the face of this great upheaval: 'We cannot provide the peasants with land to an extent where their life be made completely secure. The peasant must remember that his personal labour is his chief source of livelihood, and therefore…a too generous grant of land will instead prove morally injurious to him, relieving him of the necessity to value his labour.'[184] Under the terms of the reform, though, the Russian peasantry were amply protected from such moral peril. The aim of the government was not to provide the peasants with sufficient land to relieve them from the burden of toil, but only with that with which they could 'assure their livelihood and their fulfilment of all obligations to the government and the landowner'.[185] The emancipated peasants thus lacked both of the types of freedom by which Marx identifies the emerging proletariat in England – they were not free from, unencumbered by, any means of production of their own; nor were they personally free from obligations related to the possession of those means of production.

In order to understand the production relations of the peasants after emancipation, and up to the revolution – and therefore to determine the extent, if any, of the transition to a capitalist economic structure – we need to look at the extent of peasant holdings and the nature of their control over both the means of production and their own labour power.

The Size of Peasant Allotments After 1861

Peasant allotments under the emancipation settlement ranged from 2.5 acres up to 32.4 acres per soul (adult male), depending on the quality of the soil.[186] In total the 1861 Reform distributed 91.8 million acres of arable land between 10,050,000 'souls'[187] at an average of 9.1 acres per soul.

Even with the burdens of redemption payments and of the continuing obligations to former landlords, the majority of emancipated peasants received into their possession an amount of land sufficient for the realisation of their means of subsistence.[188] Land allotments for the 2 million crown serfs and the 19 million state serfs (emancipated in 1863 and 1866 respectively) were even greater, averaging 8-12 acres for various categories of former crown serfs and 16.2 acres for former state serfs. The allotments 'received' by this latter group remained the property of the state and these peasants were classed as 'tenant occupiers' until 1886 when their annual rents were converted to redemption payments, and the land they occupied became peasant property.

While it is generally true that those who received less than average-sized allotments did so because their land was of better than average quality, a significant number of former serfs received a negligible amount of land and some received no land at all. Lyashchenko estimates a total of 2.8 million peasants who received no land or a negligible amount of land under the terms of the emancipation.[189]

Keen to argue for the existence of a significant proletariat in pre-1917 Russia, Lyashchenko overstates the size of this collection of landless workers as a proportion of the population, suggesting that his total of 2,804,000 amounted to 11 per cent of the peasantry. Actually, this figure amounted to 11 per cent of the *former serfs of private landlords*, or 5.2 per cent of the peasantry. Lyashchenko also quotes Lokhtin's estimate of 2.6 million 'rendered landless by the reform' in support of his figures and rounds his total up to 4 million by the addition of 1 million 'workers with land allotments of less than one dessyatin'[190] (2.7 acres). Many of those receiving such small allotments, though, were recipients of 'gratuitous allotments', one-quarter the size of the local maximum, but with no redemption payments attached. Often those who opted for this small but free allotment were the second males in households which lacked the labour power to work two larger allotments efficiently enough to pay two sets of redemption fees.[191] Such minimal allotments should not therefore be blindly treated as insufficient plots.[192] Even taking Lyashchenko's most generous estimates, though, 4 million landless peasants and workers still amounts to less than 5.5 per cent of the population of Russia in 1861. Lyashchenko's claim of proletarian status for these landless workers is further compromised by the 15 per cent of poorer peasants who, by choice or under pressure from landowners, remained in a state of 'temporary obligation' throughout the 1860s. These peasants, 'still serfs in all but name'[193] continued to pay *obrok* (rent in kind or money) or *barschina* (labour-dues) under the pre-reform system for up to 20 years after the reform. Their numbers, however, had dwindled to 1 million by 1881 when the law of 28 December ordered their transfer to the status of 'redemption paying proprietors' as of 1 January1883.[194]

The amount of land held as peasant allotments increased from 91.8 million acres in 1861 to 315 million in 1877 and 332 million by 1905. Most of this later increase is accounted for by the government sponsored migration to Siberia from 1885. Under this scheme 1,094,000 peasants crossed the Urals by 1900 to receive 40.5 acres per soul 'for perpetual use', in return for an annual rent. The peasant population also increased its landholdings through the acquisition of non-allotment lands. The purchase of such land by peasants was possible after 1861, and was actively encouraged after the formation of the Peasant Land Bank in 1882.[195] By 1905 67 million acres (nearly 24 per cent of all privately held land in Russia) was owned by peasants[196] and a further 80 million acres was leased by peasants, mostly from the landowning nobility.[197] A total of 495 million acres of land was, then, under peasant cultivation of some sort by 1905, at an average of 41.25 acres per household.

It is, of course, true that many peasant households had to survive on considerably less than this generous average. The 1905 agrarian census gives figures for the distribution of *allotment* land among peasant households showing that the majority were able to meet their subsistence requirements from their possession of this land.[198]

While the transfer of allotment lands was restricted by a host of regulations and conditions and prohibited by law between 1893 and 1906, the major reason for the differences between the range of allotment sizes at emancipation (2.5 acres – or 1.8 for a 'gratuitous allotment' – to 32.4 acres) and those given here for 1905 was the repartitioning process carried out in the vast majority of peasant communes. This process took account of quality of land, size of household and number of households in the commune. It seems reasonable to suggest, then, that – to some extent at least – the range in the sizes of holdings revealed in these figures illustrates not so much the stratification of the peasantry, but the range in the requirements of different households, in terms of the size of the household and the quality of land available. The point here is not to suggest that the repartitioning process was so successful that there was only negligible inequality among the Russian peasantry (in terms of their possession of allotment holdings). Rather, the aim is to emphasise the fact that without consideration of the size of household or the quality of land, the different quantities of allotment land are not necessarily an accurate guide to the relative poverty or affluence of different households. As the largest allotments were allocated to the largest households, and in the least fertile areas, it should be safe to assume that the picture presented by the bare statistics overstates the degree of stratification.

According to the figures from the 1905 census, 84.2 per cent of peasant households were in possession of allotment lands of over 10.8 acres and 50.5 per cent enjoyed holdings of more than twice that amount.[199] Ten acres was certainly not a generous area but was sufficient in most circumstances for independent subsistence, especially given that the vast majority of the lower acreage allotment holdings were in the most fertile districts of the Black Soil region, districts which were selling areas in the internal market. The potential for independent farming was further increased by the 67 million acres of land privately owned by the peasants, and the 80 million acres of land leased by that class. This land amounted to 28 per cent of all peasant cultivated land in 1905, and is not included in the census figures. (No figures are available for the distribution of this non-allotment land.)

Excluding leased land, the average peasant household cultivated 36.15 acres of arable land in 1905, compared to 38.26 acres prior to emancipation. These figures may be somewhat misleading, though, as, according to Robinson's estimates,[200] the number of individual peasants rose by more than the number of peasant households between 1860 and 1905. He estimates a peasant population of 84 million in 1905 compared to 50 million in 1860. On these figures the decrease in the amount of land *per peasant* would have been absorbed by increasing productivity, from an annual average of 450-525 kg/ha for the first 70 years of the nineteenth century, to 615 kg/ha for 1905.[201] Taken together, the increase in productivity and the decrease in land per peasant return annual 'output per peasant' figures of 5730-6733 kg up to 1870, and 6273 kg for 1905.

The agrarian census of 1905 was the last national survey of landholding in the Russian Empire to give any indication as to the distribution of land among various sizes of peasant holdings. A series of local surveys carried out in four *uezds* (counties) in diverse areas of European Russia between 1910 and 1912 provides the only evidence of this kind for the period from 1905 to the collapse of the Tsarist regime.[202] While it's impossible to judge how representative these areas were of the situation elsewhere in Russia, none of the *uezds* in these studies were in the Steppe region, where land productivity was lowest and allotments largest. (Also these surveys refer only to allotment land, and make no reference to privately owned or leased land.) Accordingly, it may safely be assumed that productivity in the areas surveyed was higher than the national average and thus that a lower required acreage for independent subsistence farming pertained. This is particularly true of the Gadiach and Vladimir-Volynskii *uezds*, located in the fertile Black Soil region. In these two areas, the 'small holdings' were denoted as those with less than one dessyatin (2.7 acres) of arable allotment. Over 90 per cent of landed households in these *uezds* possessed a larger holding. In the other two studies, holdings of up to three dessyatins (8.1 acres) were distinguished from those with more than that amount. In these districts, 97.8 per cent of households with land fell into the latter category. The number of landless households among the total of 105,594 households across all four studies was 4714. At 4.5 per cent this was roughly the same proportion of the peasantry as indicated by Lyashchenko's largest estimates of landlessness in the 1860s.

In terms of the national (empire-wide) situation the estimates collected by G.T. Robinson suggest that by 1914 12.5 million peasant households 'possessed', in one form or another, more than 460.2 million acres, at an average of over 36.8 acres per household. (The amount of land leased by peasants is not known, nor are any figures given for the distribution of land among various sizes of holding.)

It is unlikely, though, that this situation, even by 1917, was significantly different from that in 1905. Under the terms of the Stolypin land reforms peasants were able to apply to have their allotment lands transferred into their private ownership, and to formally separate from the commune. Land so transferred was then eligible for sale to other peasants or to the Peasant Land Bank. Lyashchenko remarks that 'the Stolypin Reform achieved the unmistakable result of hastening the proletarianisation process in the village on the one hand, and of consolidating the position of the strong kulak elements on the other'.[203] While many of the better-off peasants were no doubt encouraged by Stolypin's attempt to foster a bourgeois understanding of property rights among the peasantry, the amount of land which actually changed hands in this period was negligible. By 1914 less than 10 per cent of peasant land had been transferred from allotment status to private property, and only 2.3 per cent of the total land in the possession of the peasants in 1905 had changed hands from peasant to peasant.[204] This 2.3 per cent of land was sold by 9.6 per cent of the peasantry, which suggests that the majority of selling peasants were among the 15.8 per cent of households whose allotment land had amounted to less than 10.8 acres in 1905.[205] A government commission into land tenure and sales reported that at least one-third of those who sold land during this period (in 12 sample counties of European Russia) did so in order to resettle elsewhere, as independent farmers.[206] Perhaps then, 6-7 per cent, or around 800,000 of the 12 million peasant households of 1905, had fallen into landlessness during the era of the Stolypin reforms.

These figures cannot be taken as anything more than a very rough estimate, but they are calculated from the same sources which Soviet historians have used to present the effects of Stolypin's measures as a massive boost to the kulak class on the one hand, and on the other, a wholesale proletarianisation of the poorer peasants, forced by economic necessity to sell their lands to the kulaks, and to head for the factories. The limited nature of the statistics on peasant land ownership poses serious problems for the analysis of economic differentiation within that class up to 1917. Insofar as figures do exist, however, they do not point to a significant stratum of impoverished peasants forced to (and able to) turn, for their survival, to permanent industrial wage labour. Nor had wage labour penetrated the agrarian economy to any significant extent. The vast majority of Russian peasants continued to work the land, under a variety of arrangements, of which permanent, full-time wage labour was of minimal numerical significance.[207]

This section has largely focused on quantitative aspects of peasants' land holdings. The following section examines the qualitative character of the various relations of ownership and possession from emancipation to 1917.

The Terms of the Peasants' control over Means of Production and Labour Power 1861-1917

Under the terms of the emancipation settlement, the land which passed into the possession of the peasants did not pass into their private *ownership* or their full, effective *control*. That is, they did not gain the full set of ownership rights which are generally associated with the concept of private property, or the set of powers indicated by the concept of effective control.

The reforms of the 1860s attempted to strengthen the peasants' belief in the communal nature of peasant landownership by confirming the re-allotting and equalising functions of the peasant commune – the *Mir*. The vast majority of communes continued, periodically, to redistribute land among their member households after the reforms. This was facilitated under the emancipation settlement by placing the responsibility for the payment of redemption fees with the commune, not with the individual peasants or households. As most allotment land was subject to periodic reassessment and re-allocation by the commune administration, peasant possession of this land was necessarily and transparently temporary, and their ownership (and control), therefore, was incomplete. In addition to the power to allocate arable and common land among different families, the village assembly was able to permit or prohibit the sub-division of land allocations within households.

In some circumstances it was theoretically possible for a household to claim and purchase its 'share' of the commune land, and also to sell any land so acquired. The regulations governing the rights of former serfs to buy and sell such lands, though, varied according to the type of commune, the province – or even the district – in which it was located, the amount of the redemption fees already paid, the number and extent of repartitions since emancipation and a host of local considerations, such as whether or not the 'house and garden' plot or the pasture and forest lands were included in repartitions. Any study of these conditions illustrates that even in the most favourable circumstances it was extremely difficult, in practice, for a peasant to purchase allotment lands, especially as this involved separation from the commune, and thus a further set of obstacles to be overcome.

Communal responsibility for redemption fees and other debts 'gave the commune a powerful motive to retain its redemption paying members, thus inhibiting the mobility of the individual peasant, despite his emancipation from direct obligation to the landowner'.[208] Robinson argues that:

membership [of the commune] and allotment holding were inseparable. So long as the land remained in repartitional tenure, it was the duty and the right of the commune to offer the allotment – and it was the right and the duty of the householder to receive it; so it had to be, if the system of repartition were to operate when the allotment was a burden as well as when it was an asset.[209]

Membership and allotment holding were so closely inter-related that leaving the commune and alienating the land were necessarily processes which could not be completed separately, and therefore 'any difficulty in the way of either of these operations was...at the same time an obstacle to the other'.[210] Under the terms of the emancipation, the peasant's relation to his means of production was thus intimately bound up with his control – or lack of control – over his labour power and his person.

Even after 1870, when the village assembly lost the right to prevent a member from separating from the commune and transferring his land to another, several restrictions remained. First, the potential separator had to pay off his redemption debt in full, or find a purchaser who would take on the land with its obligations. (As the value of the land was frequently less than the redemption debt this was a major obstacle.) Further, the purchaser had to be approved as a new member by the commune, and the separator had to show that another commune had voted in favour of receiving him as a registered member. Any outstanding debts and taxes against the separator also had to be met before the transfer could take place. Full separation from the commune was thus a difficult and often impossible operation, and even temporary absences (to work in industry over the winter, for example) required a passport which the commune was under no obligation to issue.

The first major revisions of the regulations governing the purchase and sale of peasant allotments came in 1881 and 1882. In addition to the reductions in redemption fees and the abolition of the state of 'temporary obligation' these years saw the removal of all official means for the transfer of hereditary allotments which had not been fully redeemed. This situation continued until 1895 when further restrictions were placed on the transfer of peasant property[211] again reducing the peasant's control over his means of production. From December 1893 the sale and mortgage of peasant allotments was prohibited, and non-allotment land belonging to peasants, even if fully paid for, could only be sold to other peasants. The laws of 1893 also explicitly stated that the holder of the limited ownership rights in peasant land could not be an individual, but was always a household. Thus it was possible for peasants to bequeath or inherit only via the mechanism of the 'election' of a new head of the household on the death of the former head. As almost all communes assigned that status to the oldest non-senile male, the election was generally a formality.

With selling, mortgaging and bequeathing all severely restricted, the most common form of transfer of peasant property was through family or household division. This too was legally restricted, requiring the agreement of the head of the household and two-thirds of the village assembly. In practice, though, this was the method of transfer which was most easily achieved outside of the legal procedures and the number of peasant households increased by nearly 50 per cent between 1860 and 1905. (From 8.5 million to 12 million.)

From the emancipation in the 1860s to the early years of the twentieth century, then, the general trend in the laws governing peasant 'ownership' of land was in the direction of increasing regulation and restriction and diminishing peasant control. It has already been noted that temporary absence from the commune required the permission of the village assembly and that permanent resettlement away from the commune was inhibited by the close connection between membership of the commune and allotment holding. (And that such resettlement would constitute only movement from one commune to another, rather than from commune to independence.) These restrictions, which remained in place right up until 1906, excluded the peasantry from proletarian status by denying the individual peasant the right and power to sell his labour power on the market, as a commodity. That is: the peasant was denied significant elements of legal ownership and effective control over both his labour power and his person. In addition, there was widespread possession of the means of production by peasants, and that possession was feudal in character (i.e. the peasants' rights and powers were generally sufficient for the realisation of their means of subsistence, but were significantly less than those associated with the ownership of private property under capitalism).

From 1903 there was a reversal of this trend and, between then and 1917, extensive steps were taken by the Tsarist regime to promote a bourgeois approach to property and ownership amongst the peasantry. The abolition of the collective responsibility of the commune for the debts of its members in 1903 was a significant move in this direction. While this measure did little to dissolve the close relationship between commune-membership and allotment holding, it did remove one of the most important motives for communes to inhibit separation by their members. The practical effects of this legislation were negligible, though, until 1906 when two further acts ruled that peasants were allowed to live permanently in cities and were no longer compelled to register with a commune (a new status of 'member at large' was introduced), and that peasant property was allowed to be held as individual, rather than household, property

Taken together, the legislation of 1903 and 1906 considerably reduced the obstacles in the path of would be separators. These potential separators generally fell into one of two categories. On the one hand, there were holders of inadequate allotments wishing to leave the commune in order to pursue wage labour, on the other hand better-off 'kulak' peasants, often with substantial holdings outside of the commune, seeking to free their allotment land from the restrictions of the commune and the primitive production methods inherent in strip farming.

In both cases separators moved closer to capitalist class locations, either as landless labourers or as petty-proprietors or petty-bourgeois farmers. For the first time Russian peasants could gain the personal freedom associated with the bourgeois era. Equality before the law with other classes (1905) and the abolition of corporal punishment contributed to the peasants' own sense of increasing liberty, but the freedoms which really had the potential to propel the peasants towards capitalist relations were those which allowed them to opt out of the communal system and to sell their labour power to the highest bidder. The 1903 legislation had freed them from responsibility for the debts of other peasants, 1906 saw the promotion of individual property rights and the measures of the Stolypin reforms from 1907 to 1912 gave the peasants the opportunity to withdraw their allotment holdings from communal administration and to gain full bourgeois ownership rights over that property.

Thus, by the last years of the Empire, the formal provisions were in place for Russia's peasantry to begin to move towards capitalist relations, either as landless proletarians – as wage labourers free from feudal (and communal) restrictions and free from ownership of any means of production, or as rural petty-proprietors or small capitalist farmers. However, the establishment of formal mechanisms and the emergence of actual capitalist relations are quite different things and by 1917 the vast majority of Russian peasants continued to obtain their means of subsistence by working commune-bound allotment land, and to remain subject to communal restrictions on their movement and employment.

Yet the progressive legislation introduced between 1903 and 1912 did have some effect. Peasants who had long worked in mines and factories away from the commune now had the right to do so regardless of the say of the village assembly. Others who had been prevented from doing such work by the commune could no longer be legally so restrained. Better-off peasants were able to extract their allotment holdings from communal regulation and to consolidate that land into their (generally larger) non-allotment land. Landowners as well as industrialists benefitted from the new relations which made the employment of free wage-labour a legal and to some extent practical possibility.

The Emerging Proletariat in Pre-revolutionary Russia

In order to assess the extent of the development of a proletariat it is necessary to consider two aspects of the production relations of the producers: the control which they held over their own labour power and that which they held over means of production. It has already been shown that the majority of Russian producers were in possession of sufficient means of production to realise their means of subsistence without selling their labour power to capitalist employers. This section will deal with the remaining workers in Tsarist Russia – those engaged in wage labour. The central concerns here are the extent to which wage labourers could be considered *free* wage-labourers' (i.e. proletarians) and the size of the proletariat relative to the number of non-proletarian producers in Russia.

The Rural Proletariat

According to the 1897 census, 1.8 million peasants were permanently employed in agricultural wage labour. Hugh Seaton-Watson suggests that 'if family dependents are included the number affected would be at least doubled',[212] amounting to 2.8 per cent of the population. Although these workers were not free wage-labourers in 1897, the reforms of the Stolypin era brought proletarian freedoms to some such workers.

Often, though, the wages of these workers contributed to a household dominated by non-wage incomes. In cases where the income from wage labour was not sufficient to be viable outside of the household context, the nominally free wage-labourers would lack the properties of mobility and fluidity which form a large part of the reason why free wage labour is the ideal – and necessary – dominant production relation under capitalism. Thus, while we may consider all of these permanent free wage labourers to be individually proletarian in character, we should be cautious of employing these figures as a measure of the advance of capitalism in pre-revolutionary Russia. Notwithstanding this reservation, it should be safe to say that the number of proletarian agricultural labourers and their family dependents amounted to less than 4 million persons, or 2.8 per cent of the population in 1897. It is not possible to calculate exactly the growth (or decline) in the size of this 'rural proletariat' in the 20 years from 1897 to the revolution, yet some indicators are available. If the results of the four studies carried out in the last years before the war (see above) are taken as representative of the Empire as a whole, the number of agricultural wage labourers on peasant lands would amount to around 2 million. (One agricultural wage labourer per 25 households, applied to the 12.5 million peasant households in 1914.)[213] At this time, 82 per cent of land actually cultivated was in the hands of the peasants. The number of wage labourers on the remaining 18 per cent of cultivated land is not known, but various factors suggest that the degree of wage labour was no higher on non-peasant land than on peasant land. The vast majority of the former belonged to private landlords and while it would seem logical to assume that the degree of wage labour would have been higher on the larger estates of the landlords than on the lands of the peasants, two factors mitigate against such a situation:

1. Outside of a small number of estates, the private landowners were unable and unwilling to embrace capitalistic agriculture. The majority of the estates of the nobility continued to practise some form of feudal or semi-feudal agriculture right up to the revolution. As late as 1900, 71 per cent of estates mortgaged at the 'Nobleman's Bank' received labour-dues or rent in kind from the peasants who worked their land.
2. The more progressive landlords were also those employing what mechanisation there was in Russian agriculture before the revolution, reducing the labour requirements per acre of

a major potential source of proletarian rural employment.

It is unlikely, then, that the number of agricultural wage labourers per acre on private estates was much higher than on peasant lands, and indeed the number could well have been lower. Even if the rate of agricultural wage labour on private lands had been twice that found on peasant lands, the total number of such workers would have been no more than 2.5 million. While this would represent an increase of 0.7 million since 1897, the rate of increase would only be equal to that of the general population growth. The percentage of the population engaged in agricultural wage labour, by these (probably over-generous) calculations would be 1.42, both in 1897 and in 1914.

The Industrial Proletariat

According to official Soviet histories, the Russian working class had, by 1890, become 'a contemporary industrial proletariat, entirely unlike the earlier workers of the semi-feudal factories or the small-scale kustars and other manual producers'.[214] Leaving aside for a moment the question of the size of the industrial workforce, it is interesting to note the Soviet treatment of the *character* of the Russian working class in the last years of the nineteenth century. Lyashchenko argues that by the 1890s, 65 per cent of the labour force in the Donets mines consisted of permanent workers. This figure rises to 89 per cent in the St Petersburg region, and to 97 per cent in the metalworking industries across the Empire.[215] A similar impression is given by the 1893 report of the Ministry of Finance inspector for Moscow, which suggested that 82 per cent of factory workers in that region were permanent urban residents. Yet figures from most other sources present a significantly different picture.

In direct contrast to Lyashchenko, John Keep asserts that 'as late as 1913 the overwhelming majority of Donets miners returned home in summer to help with the harvest'.[216] A survey of 1913, published in 1917 by V.P. Miliutin, suggested that, even among the skilled printing trades in Moscow, 46 per cent of workers were still personally involved in farming on their own land, and a further 16.7 per cent were members of rural landed households[217]. While it is impossible to establish even a rough estimate of the proportion of industrial workers across the Empire who maintained a given level of involvement in the village – or held an amount of land sufficient to threaten their proletarian status – it is clear that the size of the industrial proletariat did not directly equate to the size of the industrial workforce.

It is especially worth noting that the overwhelming majority of industrial workers retained peasant status until the last years before the revolution. Hans Rogger estimates that in 1900, 90 per cent of urban workers were still designated as peasants in their passports.[218] The legal and actual restrictions on the personal freedoms of the peasants before 1905 have already been noted. These restrictions diminished the workers' control over their own labour power as much for industrial workers as for those who remained on the land. Only after the Stolypin reforms did any peasant workers achieve the freedoms associated with the proletarian wage labourer.

The difficulties involved in arriving at even a rough estimate of the proportion of industrial workers who could be considered to be of proletarian status may not prove to be too great an inconvenience to the analysis of the extent of capitalist development in Tsarist Russia. For, as in the case of the rural proletariat, it is possible to always accept the figures which suggest the greatest extent of proletarianisation, and still to find that the proletariat accounted for less than 10 per cent of Russia's population in the last years before the revolution.

Official Soviet figures estimate the number of industrial workers in 1914 at 4.3 million, or nearly 9 million if family dependents are included. These are nearly double the estimates of other historians, yet even the Soviet figures find industrial workers and their families to constitute only 5.1 per cent of the population. The addition of the 2.5 million agricultural wage labourers and their families (again the highest estimate) brings this figure up to 7.4 per cent. Both domestic servants and 'other ranks' members of the armed forces are referred to by Marx as 'wage labourers not employed as such' and it could be argued that those in such employment should be accorded proletarian status. The addition of the 1.5 million soldiers and sailors in service at the outbreak of the war, and around 1.2 million domestic servants, would further increase the number of wage labourers up to 15.7 million, or 8.9 per cent of the population.

Thus, even when the most generous estimates are employed at every opportunity, it remains impossible to escape the conclusion that less than one Russian in ten realised their means of subsistence via proletarian free wage labour. More conservative estimates suggest a considerably lower proportion of proletarians, perhaps as low as one in 20 or even one in 25. The failure of capitalist production relations to penetrate the lives of the mass of ordinary Russian producers was matched by the failure of Russia's 'non-productive classes' to embrace capitalist relations or a capitalist mode of production.

The Bourgeoisie and the Nobility

With the continuing dominance of pre-capitalist production relations, the Russian bourgeoisie remained weak and ineffective, unable to extend the capitalist mode of production into the lives of the Russian masses. The nobility, whose English counterparts had done much to hasten capitalist development by placing their operations on a capitalist footing, and by evictions and enclosures, were largely unwilling or unable to embrace bourgeois production relations. Robert Edelman suggests that at the time of the emancipation 'most nobles were ill-equipped to handle the transition to controlling a relatively free labour market and managing a commercial farm. Most Russian landlords actually knew little about agronomy, food processing or animal husbandry. They lacked the necessary capital and the majority of them still considered service, not farming, to be their true career.'[219]

Edelman notes that the common historical description of the nobility as a class in decline, while substantially correct, omits 'important countervailing trends'.[220] He identifies a 'provincial landowning gentry in the best eighteenth-century English sense',[221] opposing this concept to that of a 'landed bourgeoisie in the real sense of the term'.[222] Edelman's characterisation of this group derives from his view that their continuing allegiance to traditional notions of 'honour, service and family' could not be considered the 'prototypical behaviour of the agricultural entrepreneur'.[223] From an historical materialist perspective, though, these behavioural traits are of secondary importance. The bourgeois character of these 'progressive' landlords is measured in terms of their development of capitalist production. Edelman acknowledges the attempts of these landlords to 'exploit their own lands and to produce by efficient means for the market', and that contemporary agricultural journals sometimes referred to a 'managerial revolution' in the Russian countryside.[224] Yet, for all this, the number of landlords orienting their production towards cash crops and employing wage labour was not sufficient to make a major impact on the overall character of Russian agriculture. The landholdings of the noble families, in decline since emancipation, represented less than 18 per cent of cultivated Russia by 1914. While the owners of the largest latifundia lacked the need or the desire to introduce capitalistic production, most estimates suggest that around 75 per cent of noble estates lacked the capital necessary for modernisation in that direction.[225] As Rogger notes, 'the average estate was as backward and under-capitalised as most peasant farms and did little to justify official hopes that the gentry would serve as teachers of advanced methods of cultivation'.[226] Beyond the agrarian sphere, in industry and commerce, the bourgeoisie also struggled to establish itself as a progressive force in the social and economic life of Tsarist Russia. Walkin argues that:

> Russia did not develop a middle class similar to the powerful middle classes of the west. Those concerned with trade and industry were small in number, largely illiterate until the end of the nineteenth century, and dependent on the state. It is characteristic that the state itself attempted to create an organised middle class and urban self-government, but without success.[227]

The Russian state's attempts to modernise social and political life, though, appear half-hearted and piecemeal compared to its involvement in the economy. Under successive finance ministers (Vyshnegradsky, 1887-1892 and Witte, 1892-1903) the government undertook 'energetic and comprehensive' measures to develop domestic industry.[228] Such was the extent of government involvement in the economy that John Keep has noted that 'many features of the "planned economy" instituted after 1917 had pre-revolutionary antecedents'. Keep adds that 'as a force independent of the state, Russian capitalism never really got off the ground'.[229] In addition to protective customs tariffs (from 1891) and the adoption of the gold standard (1897) the government provided loans, subsidies and other incentives to domestic industrialists, protected various industries from foreign competition, financed strategic industries and created an 'ersatz market'[230] by entering into long-term fixed-price purchase agreements, particularly in railway related industries. In 1890, the state owned 24 per cent of Russia's 21,000 versts of railway track.[231] By 1902 state ownership had risen to 67 per cent of a total of 53,000 versts.[232] In addition to the lines under full state ownership, the government held substantial interests in all of the six companies which between them controlled 80 per cent of the privately owned railways in Russia.[233] The government-backed railway boom gave a strong impetus to the Russian metallurgical industries, and again the state was the largest and most important customer, taking two-thirds of total output in 1899.[234]

Government purchase of industrial goods was facilitated by the growth of large industry *combines* which were officially encouraged from the turn of the century. The *Prodameta*, formed in 1902, represented all of the large metallurgical producers and sold to the state at inflated prices. The *Produgol* (1904, coal), *Prodvagon* (1904, rail wagons), *Prodarud* (1907, iron-ore) and *Med* (1907, copper) were all formed to assist state purchases, and in all cases the state was willing to pay above market prices in order to encourage industrial development.[235]

The state assisted development, not only as a purchaser of industrial goods, but also in its role as an investor. Until the late 1880s, the state bank was the major provider of credit to Russian businesses. Lyashchenko suggests that 'the political weakness of the bourgeoisie, frightened by the movement of the working class and dependent upon government orders, reduced it to a position of subservience to Tsarism and into an alliance with it'.[236] Furthermore, 'The general social-economic backwardness of Russia contributed to keeping the nation in the position of a major appendage to the Western imperialist powers...both the Tsarist regime and Russian capitalism were inextricably dependent upon foreign capital.'[237] By 1914, 42.6 per cent of basic stock capital in the 18 largest corporate banks in Russia was foreign owned. According to Lyashchenko, the large Russian industrial combines 'did not play an independent, active role in the world wide struggle for territory among the capitalist trusts. They were, in fact, themselves frequently the object of precisely such a struggle among the foreign imperialist systems for the exploitation of Russia.'[238]Lyashchenko sees the involvement of the state in the economy and the influence of foreign capital on Russian development as inextricably linked: 'First, the financial oligarchy frequently became a financial oligarchy of foreign capital, owing to the dependence of the leading Russian banks on foreign finance, and second, it frequently merged with the oligarchy of Russia's military feudal imperialism and its financial bureaucratic apparatus to become the executor of the will of the same foreign imperialist capitalism.'[239] Foreign investment in Russia had increased from less than 10 million roubles in 1860 to 1750 million roubles by 1914, accounting for around one-third of company assets in Russia. Over half of this foreign capital was concentrated in mining and the metallurgical industries, where it accounted for 90 per cent and 40 per cent of investment. Other important targets of foreign investors were the banks, where non-Russian capital accounted for 43 per cent of credit, and the textile industry, with 28 per cent of assets foreign owned.[240]

The importance of the extent of foreign investment in Russia on domestic political developments remains debatable.[241] For our present purposes, though, the extensive involvement of the state in economic development and the reliance of the Russian economy on foreign capital serve to illustrate the weakness of the domestic bourgeoisie as an independent force.

Capitalist Development in Russia up to 1917

To what extent then, did the economic structure evident in Russia in 1917 resemble Marx's conception of capitalism? The foremost measure of capitalist development, in historical materialist terms, is that of the character of the economic structure – the sum of production relations. As has been shown, capitalist production relations had penetrated the lives of no more than 10 per cent of Russian producers by the time of the Bolshevik revolution. The vast majority of immediate producers fell outside of Marx's conception of proletarian status, either by virtue of their possession of significant means of production or because of their insufficient control over their own labour power.

The 'expropriation of the great mass of the people from the soil, from the means of subsistence'[242] had not yet taken place. The means of production had not yet been 'transformed from the pygmy property of the many into the huge property of the few'.[243] The absence of these fundamental aspects of the capitalist economic structure restricted the development of the capitalist mode of production. Labour obligations were becoming less common but remained in place for a significant proportion of producers, illustrating the continuing presence of the feudal mode of exploitation and form of surplus labour. Production for the accumulation of capital was not typical, and what there was, was largely concentrated in enterprises funded by foreign capital.

3.2 Lenin – War Communism and the NEP

Having illustrated the absence of any significant manifestations of capitalism in pre-revolutionary Russia before the Bolshevik revolution, it is now necessary to turn to the post-revolutionary period. The Soviet era is often viewed in terms of the attempt to build socialism in Russia, and the success or failure in meeting that goal provides the focus for many studies in Soviet history. The argument which will be presented in this section is that a view of the Soviet period as an attempt to build socialism in Russia, while valid, is less profitable than a view of the Soviet era as a series of measures, often undertaken as forced and even resented reactions to unfavourable circumstances, which were to result, eventually, in the establishment of the economic conditions required for the transition to capitalism. This is not to say, of course, that the Soviet regimes did not wish to build socialism, nor that some of their policies could have, under different circumstances, contributed to the achievement of that goal. (i.e. those measures may have been communistic in character and may even have brought the economic structure of

Soviet Russia closer to communism. But, in the *given historical circumstances*, the combined effect of these measures was to hasten the advent of capitalism in Russia.)

As stated earlier, the fundamental process of the transition from feudalism to capitalism is the transformation of the economic structure. Under the feudal economic structure, producers and non-producers hold different rights and powers over both the labour power of the producers and some of the means of production. In contrast, the capitalist economic structure is characterised by the concentration of ownership and control of the means of production in the hands of non-producers. Most producers hold no relevantly significant means of production, but hold full ownership rights over their own labour power. The process of expropriation and of concentration of ownership of the land which constitutes the movement from a feudal economic structure to a capitalist one forms, for Marx, 'the prelude to the history of capital'[244]. Yet, as has been shown, land ownership in Russia at the time of the revolution was dominated by feudal hangovers, small-scale ownership and petty production. Before capitalism could emerge in Russia, the peasants would have to be relieved of their possession of the land and freed from any obligations connected to that possession.

Marx had expected that communist revolutionaries, having seized political power, would be faced with the task of socialising the means of production from a state of concentration in the hands of a minority capitalist class, and that the working classes, in such a situation, would already enjoy the full ownership and control of their own labour power associated with proletarian status. This was not the situation facing the Bolsheviks in 1917. The pre-1914 predominance of petty-proprietorship and small-scale production on the land had been further removed from capitalistic conditions by the Tsarist regime's war measures, particularly their imposition of a state monopoly on grain purchases. The Provisional Government's attempts to feed the towns and the army had also amounted, in practice, to grain requisitioning. These measures were deeply resented and regularly resisted by the peasants. By the time of the Bolshevik seizure of power, food shortages were acute and trade on the black market was widespread.

War Communism 1917-1921

The backwardness of pre-revolutionary Russia, compounded by the chaos of war since 1914, profoundly affected the ways in which the Bolshevik regime was able to attempt to move forwards into socialism. While any seizure of power in the name of the proletariat might be expected to provoke civil war and counter-revolution, the Bolsheviks had to meet these challenges from a position far removed from that expected by Marx.

The set of policies adopted by the Bolshevik regime in its early years came to be known collectively as 'War Communism'. Alec Nove suggests that War Communism had two inter-related causes – the ideological presuppositions of the Bolsheviks, and the state of war emergency that faced them until the last months of 1921.[245] Nove further suggests that the latter was used to justify the more extreme manifestations of the former.[246] Yet it is clear that the extreme circumstances that the Bolsheviks found themselves in contributed in large measure to the extreme policies with which they began to attempt to construct socialism, and to their success or otherwise in implementing these policies. Nove acknowledges that, during the War Communism period, 'real life at no time conformed to the government's intentions'.[247]

The civil war presented the new regime with an immediate and compelling economic priority – to feed the Red Army. Under the Land Decree of 8 November 1917[248] land was nationalised (although the decree was unclear about whether this included the peasants' private household plots). The peasants retained the right to use the land, but how the land was used was to be supervised by local committees. No one was to hold more than he was able to cultivate, as the hiring of labour was forbidden. While the Soviet system has sometimes been described as 'State Capitalism', this land decree, the first major decree of the new Bolshevik regime, has more of an air of *state feudalism*. The peasant producers retained the right to occupy and use the land, but did not enjoy the full set of ownership rights characteristic of ownership in a capitalist sense. Nor did the state enjoy all of these rights over the land. The lack of clarity as to the ownership of the peasants' household plots also echoes the feudal situation in which both lord and peasant saw such land as their own. From a situation in which the rural economy was dominated by petty-proprietors, this supposed step forwards towards socialism can justifiably be viewed as a step backwards towards a feudal economic form. The peasants' control over their own labour power was also severely limited by the decree, as the hiring – and therefore also the selling – of labour was outlawed. The ambiguities of the decree's treatment of land ownership and the failure of the Bolsheviks to move more rapidly towards a socialist land settlement were due largely to their practical inability to enforce a settlement on the peasants under the chaotic circumstances of the civil war and in the face of economic and social backwardness.

Whereas Nove argues that the situation of war emergency was used to justify the 'more extreme manifestations' of the Bolsheviks' ideological presuppositions, the regime acknowledged the extent to which their ideologically motivated ambitions were limited by force of circumstances. While Lenin announced in general terms that 'Everyone agrees that the immediate introduction of socialism in Russia is impossible',[249] Bukharin and Preobrazhensky gave specific attention to the peasant question:

We must remember that we do not expropriate petty property. Its nationalization is absolutely out of the question, firstly because we would be unable ourselves to organize the scattered small scale production and secondly because the Communist Party does not wish to, and must not, offend the many millions of petty proprietors. Their conversion to socialism must take place voluntarily, by their own decision, and not by means of compulsory expropriation.[250]

This position does have some historical materialist precedent. In 1894 Engels had asserted – in the context of the situation in France and Germany – that: 'When we are in power we will not use force to expropriate the peasantry – only the landlords.'[251] But the language used by Bukharin and Preobrazhensky in the above quoted statement does suggest that they adopted this position for largely practical reasons – the Bolsheviks simply did not have the power to enforce a settlement on the peasants. Indeed, the Bolsheviks were forced to ally with the Social Revolutionaries even to issue the Land Decree. The clauses of the decree reflected this compromise, and were 'framed in response to peasant demands [voiced through the Social Revolutionaries] rather than in conformity with Bolshevik doctrine about the Socialization of agriculture'.[252]

The implementation of the measures announced in the Land Decree saw further compromise. Nove notes that, 'Lenin was wise enough to leave land distribution in peasant hands. Even though he would have preferred to set up state or collective farms he knew that this was quite impracticable in the circumstances.'[253] And elsewhere he goes further: 'Neither the Bolsheviks nor the Social Revolutionaries, nor any other political force could tell the peasants what to do.'[254] In practice, land re-allocation, following the decree, continued in much the same way as it had done in the month or so before the decree: 'This was not in fact a reform undertaken by the authorities, it was a more or less elemental act by the peasants, with government organs accepting, and by implication, legitimising what was happening.'[255]

Wiles rejects this idea of a regime reacting to circumstances and claims that the situation of war emergency was only later used as an excuse for policies determined all along by Bolshevik ideology.[256] But, as has been noted, leading Bolsheviks cited the extraordinary circumstances of the time as the motivation for many of the policy elements of War Communism. And we do not need to rely on these statements – the regular failure of the Bolsheviks to adopt policies in line with their ideological position and their frequent inability to implement those policies which they sought to pursue suggest, as Maurice Dobb has argued, that the regime did not plan or intend War Communism, but that their approach was constructed piecemeal, as a series of responses to war, hunger and chaos.[257]

It is true that some of the Bolsheviks saw War Communism as a positive set of policies – if not the implementation of communism, then as a step in the right direction. L.N. Kritsman, in *The Heroic Period of the Russian Revolution*, saw War Communism as a form of 'natural-anarchistic economy' and 'not a socialist form, but transitional to socialism'.[258] More typical, though, were the views of V. Firsov, who in 1923 looked back on War Communism as an unfortunate but, at the time, necessary interruption to the real Bolshevik and Soviet aim of building socialism: 'NEP was arising already in 1918...Then came the period of civil war; 'war communism' appeared. Our movement towards communism thereby slowed down, since socialist construction is impossible when all production potential is used unproductively. The war ended...The inevitable NEP appeared, the first stage of our move towards socialism.'[259] Yu Larin also cites the extreme circumstances of the period as a major cause of War Communism: 'We had to run the economy in the almost complete absence of normal economic conditions, and so inevitably the planned economy turned simply into the allocation of whatever was available.'[260]

This was particularly true of the Bolsheviks' dealings with

the peasants. Immediately following the seizure of political power, the Bolsheviks sought to forge an alliance with the peasantry – aware that they were unable to dictate terms to this, the largest section of the Russian population. Lenin's aim was to replace the pre-revolutionary state monopoly on grain purchases with a form of product exchange between worker-controlled industrial enterprises and relatively self-governing peasant petty-producers, mediated and administered by the state. Amid the chaos of war, though, the productivity of the agricultural sector was low, resulting in the peasants wanting to retain a higher proportion of their produce for themselves. This reduced the amount of grain and other agricultural produce available for willing exchange for industrial goods. Against the demands of the towns and the Red Army, the produce which the peasants viewed as 'surplus' was far from sufficient for the Bolsheviks' plans. Furthermore, with hardly any industrial production capacity allocated to producing goods which the peasants wanted or needed, the system of product exchange was very unattractive to the peasants. Not surprisingly, the black market expanded rapidly. Kritsman estimated that 60 per cent of bread grain consumed in cities during 1918 passed through illegal channels.[261] With this system of product exchange facing such severe problems, and failing to meet its objective of feeding the army and the industrial population, grain requisitioning was re-introduced by the Bolsheviks. Though this policy met with strong opposition from the peasantry, many of them, ultimately, endured the regime because they feared the whites more than they feared the Bolsheviks.

Grain requisitioning, though, provided little incentive for the peasants to increase their productivity, and the rise in state procurements of grain from 30 million poods in 1917-18 to 110 million poods in 1918-19 may have been largely due to the increasing efficiency and ruthlessness of the operation. Towards the end of 1921, recognising that agricultural recovery and development would be impossible without offering the peasants some kind of incentive to increase production, leading Bolsheviks began to speak of an alternative to requisitioning. Yet even in December of that year Lenin re-asserted the policy of requisitioning, though he signalled his unease with this approach, admitting that 'we are despots to the peasants'.[262]

In fact, the end of grain requisitioning came only when the reason for it no longer existed. When the civil war was won, there was no longer any need, or justification, for the policies of War Communism. The period of War Communism saw measures adopted in response to abnormal circumstances; the Bolsheviks quickly learnt to give up any pretensions to establishing an ideal society, and to focus all attention to a single priority – survival of the regime at any cost.

While Nove suggests that the 'force of circumstances' argument can only succeed if the ideological presuppositions of the Bolsheviks are counted among the circumstances, there actually appears to be very little evidence of the regime pursuing otherwise pointless or counter-productive measures merely for the satisfaction of ideological goals. A more important element of the 'extraordinary circumstances' which faced the Bolsheviks is the general backwardness of Russia at the time of the revolution, in terms of both the economic structure and the development of the productive forces. The fragmented and confused nature of the ownership and control of the productive forces in Russia hindered the Bolsheviks' attempts to co-ordinate the economy towards the war effort. The general economic and technological backwardness of Russia was also a major cause of the acute shortages of essential goods which characterised the period. This backwardness, in terms of the economic structure and in the level of development of the productive forces, limited the options available to the Bolsheviks. The circumstances which forced the regime to struggle from crisis to crisis were ultimately caused by the fact of Russian under-development and, in historical materialist terms, by the premature nature of the seizure of power in the name of the proletariat.

The Introduction of the New Economic Policy (NEP)

Given the desperate and chaotic conditions of the War Communism period it is perhaps not surprising that the Bolshevik regime was unable to advance significantly towards its ultimate ideological goal of building a communist society. Throughout that period the Bolsheviks adopted policies not out of ideological commitment, but out of sheer necessity. Responding to one crisis after another and fighting desperately for survival, the regime rarely had the luxury of implementing policies that derived from their ideologically driven ambitions.

Victory in the civil war, though, did little to ease this situation. By the spring of 1921 the Bolshevik regime controlled territories almost equal to the Russian Empire of 1913. (The exceptions were Poland, Finland, the Baltic States and Bessarabia.) But, with peace came demands from the Russian people for an end to the harsh policies of War Communism and to the ruthless methods employed in their implementation. Opposition to the regime was strongest among the peasantry – a serious matter in a country of over 20 million peasant households. Peasant discontent was widespread and in the autumn of 1920 open revolts broke out in many areas. (The largest of which – in the important agricultural region of Tambov – was suppressed by 50,000 Red Army troops under the command of Marshall Tukhachevsky.)

According to Nove, peasant and kulak unrest was 'leading to a situation so catastrophic that the survival of the regime came ever more clearly to depend on the relaxation of the rigours of war communism'.[263] Discussions on how to address this situation began within the party on 8 February 1921; by the seventeenth of that month the matter was under open debate within the pages of Pravda and the Central Committee had agreed to replace forcible requisitioning of grain with a tax-in-kind by the twenty-fourth.

As delegates to the Tenth Party Congress met in Petrograd the following month, the Kronstadt Rising broke out. Faced with open and armed dissent from the Kronstadt sailors – heroes of 1917 and formerly solid supporters of the Bolsheviks – Lenin knew that he could not afford to delay the move away from War Communism to a new approach to the post-civil war conditions. The party had to act quickly and decisively enough to quell the growing unease among the population.

The policies that emerged from this crisis came to be known, collectively, as the New Economic Policy, or NEP. Central to the NEP was the replacement of grain requisitioning with a tax-in-kind, set at 10 per cent, on agricultural produce. This change resulted not only in a new method for calculating the extent of the contribution to the state which was expected from the peasants, but also in a significant reduction in the overall burden placed upon them. Requisitioning quotas for 1920-21 had been set at 423 million poods for grain, 110 for potatoes and 25.4 for meat. Tax-in-kind collected in 1921-22 for those products amounted to 240, 60 and 6.5 respectively.[264]

In notes for his speech to the Tenth Party Congress Lenin considered the 'Lessons of Kronstadt: in politics – the closing of ranks (+ discipline) within the party, greater struggle against the Mensheviks and SRs; in economics – to satisfy as far as possible the middle peasantry.'[265] The reduced burden on the peasants through the tax-in-kind was a significant move towards satisfying the middle peasantry, and calming the unrest in rural areas. But the end of requisitioning was intended, also, to encourage greater productivity in agriculture, in order to ease food shortages and to allow further development of Russian industry. Most peasants were only able to trade locally, and the state was unable to arrange efficient distribution of surpluses to food deficit areas. It became necessary to legalise private trade in order to meet the objectives of relieving shortages and feeding the towns. This concession to the efficiency of the market was seen by many in the party as a retreat and in March 1921 Lenin warned the Party Congress that 'Freedom of trade...inevitably leads to white-guardism, to the victory of capital, to its full restoration.'[266] Yet private trade was legalised in that month.

Again, then, the regime was forced, by circumstances, to adopt an approach to governing Russia that was not of its own choosing – that was, in fact, abhorrent to many of the Bolsheviks and their supporters. Martin McCauley suggests that, 'If war communism was a leap into socialism, then the New Economic Policy was a leap out of socialism.'[267] Lenin, though, presented the move to NEP as a necessary tactical retreat: 'We know that so long as there is no revolution in other countries, only agreement with the peasantry can save the socialist revolution in Russia.'[268] Lenin noted the desperate condition of the country and likened Russia to 'a man beaten to within an inch of his life...it is a mercy Russia can hobble about on crutches. That is the situation we are in.'[269] In these circumstances, the direct route to the creation of a socialist society was not a viable option and the Bolsheviks had little option but to concentrate on survival, stability and development:

> There is no doubt that in a country where the overwhelming majority of the population consists of small agricultural producers, a socialist revolution can be carried out only through the implementation of a whole series of measures which would be superfluous in highly developed capitalist countries where wage workers in industry and agriculture make up the vast majority...This is not the case in Russia, for here industrial workers are a minority and petty farmers are the vast majority.[270]

NEP, then, was not an admission of defeat, but an admission that Russia was not yet ready for socialism, and that in order to survive until the advance to socialism was possible, the regime, on behalf of the proletariat, would need to appease the peasants, modernise the economy and 'cling to power so as to be able to resume the advance to communism'[271]. It was hoped that this tactical retreat would allow the regime to survive until successful revolutions in Europe could come to the aid of the Bolsheviks:

> In such a country the socialist revolution can triumph only on two conditions. First, if it is given timely support by a socialist revolution in one or several advanced countries... The second condition is agreement between the proletariat, which is exercising its dictatorship, that is, holds state power, and the majority of the peasant population.[272]

Lenin's emphasis on the importance of a co-operative link, or *smychka*, between the proletariat and a peasantry largely composed of petty-proprietors, under conditions favouring the latter, was a significant diversion from established Bolshevik policies. The extent to which the party was conceding ideological ground in the face of unfavourable circumstances is evident from Radek's admission of Menshevism at the Tenth Party Congress: 'If the Mensheviks are left at liberty now that we have adopted their policy, they will claim power; if the Social-Revolutionaries are left free, while the vast mass of the peasants are opposed to the communists, we are committing suicide.'[273]

Agriculture

The policy of appeasing the peasantry continued to be implemented and extended. Although, in March 1922, Lenin told the Eleventh Party Congress that 'the retreat is over'[274]; that there would be no new concessions to the middle peasants and kulaks. However, the Bolsheviks continued to respond to the difficulties of Russian backwardness by legalising more and more varieties of capitalistic behaviour. A decree of May 1922 allowed the peasant to 'dispose of his farm as though it belonged to him, to lease out the land, to take on paid workers'[275]. The aim of this was to enable poorer peasants to relinquish their land (which was insufficient for subsistence anyway) to middle peasants and kulaks, who would then be able to hire the newly landless labourers to work on larger, more productive farms. Free from the threat of forcible requisitioning and free to sell surpluses onto the open market, the middle peasants and kulaks would have sufficient incentive and opportunity to increase productivity. This, it was hoped, would provide the levels of agricultural output required by the regime to feed the developing urban and industrial population, and to export in exchange for desperately needed tools and machinery. In 1923, the tax-in-kind was reduced and by 1924 had been replaced by a money tax. Also in 1924, Russia's estimated 1.5 million agricultural wage workers achieved legal status, and a system of rural credit was re-established with the formation of the Agricultural Bank.

The dilemma faced by the Bolsheviks, with regard to agriculture under NEP, was that the measures outlined above, aimed at encouraging the more inventive and entrepreneurial peasants to increase productivity, also encouraged individualism and capitalistic behaviour, and increased the number of peasants who had a stake in resisting any future moves towards socialism. The development of a rural proletariat, the drift towards larger farms with ownership beginning to become concentrated in the hands of a narrow stratum of well-to-do peasants, the evolution of peasant dues into first a tax-in-kind, then a money tax, the modernisation of agrarian finances and increasing productivity, so as to be able to support the development of towns and industry, all resemble important elements in the progression from feudalism to capitalism described by Marx in the later chapters of *Capital I*, yet all were viewed by Lenin as necessary to the survival of the regime and the revolution.[276]

Lenin's strategy for guarding against the encroachment of capitalism was two-fold: to encourage co-operation (to wean the mass of the peasants from individualism), and mechanisation – to demonstrate to the peasant the advantages of socialism through the power of the tractor. While the reluctance of the regime to allow unfettered market relations presented some obstacles to the success of the ambitious peasants under NEP, prevailing material circumstances were the main barrier to the development of Russian agriculture in the early years of NEP.

A formidable barrier to progress was the obsolete system of landholding, a hangover from the pre-revolutionary period, in which the peasant, the *Mir* and representatives of the state (replacing the representatives of the landowning nobility of Tsarist times) all claimed some form of authority over the labour power and means of production of the agrarian economy. While the middle peasants and kulaks were encouraged to adopt capitalistic practices, and the very poor and landless peasants were able to sell their labour power to these entrepreneurial farmers, the mass of peasants cultivated holdings which were sufficient to provide their subsistence, but which were not sufficient to require or allow the employment of regular labour. For these peasants, NEP was intended to enable them to improve their standard of living, enough, at least, to quell any unrest, and to increase their productivity, without fostering among them too much individualism.

Lenin's attempts to promote co-operation among this section of the peasantry were successful to the extent that, by 1927, 13 million of the 25 million peasant households in the USSR were members of co-operatives[277]. Moves to encourage these peasants into collectives, though, were less successful, with state farms accounting for only 1.1 per cent of the sown area of the USSR in 1927, and collective farms accounting for just 0.6 per cent[278]. Individual household farms still dominated Soviet agriculture, with the peasant farmers involved in a variety of relationships with the village commune. For these households, the various ownership rights over the labour power of the members of the household and the means of production used by them were generally shared between the household, the *Mir* and the state, with no single body enjoying full ownership rights over any of these productive forces.

For the majority of the population of the Soviet Union, the legacy of Russia's recent feudal past continued to exert a powerful influence. Alec Nove speaks of 'an institutional setting of a semi-medieval character', suggesting that under NEP the vast majority of small-holder peasants had 'little opportunity, incentive or resources to improve their methods of production or to use machinery'[279]. Though the proportion of households leasing land more than doubled between 1922 and 1925, and those employing labour increased by 90 per cent in those years, these categories still represented only 6.1 per cent and 1.9 per cent of households by the end of that period[280]. Estimates of the kulak population vary widely, from around 3.5 per cent to 7 per cent of households, but with only 1.9 per cent of households hiring labour and, according to Lewin, only half of those employing more than one labourer,[281] the kulak class, both needed and feared by the Bolsheviks, was not significant enough to provide the surpluses required by the regime, or to pose the counter-revolutionary threat attributed to them.

The recovery of Russian agriculture was further hampered by the sheer extent of the devastation of the years of war, and by the severe famines which hit the southern and eastern regions in 1920 and 1921 (Total harvests for those years were 54 per cent and 43 per cent respectively of the 1909-1913 average. More than 3 million died and over 20 per cent of draught animals were lost in those 2 years.)[282]

All of these difficulties faced by the peasantry resulted in a drastic reduction in sowings of industrial crops (in favour of those suitable for private consumption) and also in the proportion of harvested grain finding its way to market, which dropped from around 20 per cent in 1913 to 10 per cent in 1927. The poorer households were less able to market their grain, as a larger proportion was required for subsistence, and by 1926-27 around 11 per cent of farms accounted for 56 per cent of net off-farm sales of grain. In the face of the low volume of marketed grain the government took measures to reduce the levels of private trade in agricultural products in 1925, seeking to increase its share of purchases (estimated at 75 per cent in 1925-26). Exports were the main casualty of these low marketings in the late 1920s, falling from 2 million tons in 1925 to 0.3 million in 1928, despite a slight increase in the harvest from 72.5 million tons to 73.3. (Exports in 1913 were 12 million tons, from a harvest of 80.1.)[283]

In terms of developing the rural economy, and increasing agricultural output in order to aid development of industry, then, NEP was unsuccessful. There had been a significant degree of recovery and this had eased both suffering and unrest in the countryside – enough for Lenin to declare, as early as November 1922, that 'Peasant uprisings which, before 1921 were a common occurrence in Russia, have almost completely ceased...The position of the peasant is now such that we have no reason to fear any movement against us from him.'[284] The regime had successfully achieved Lenin's prime motive for the introduction of NEP – the removal of the threat to the regime's survival presented by peasant dissatisfaction. As has been shown above, attempts to encourage co-operation among the peasantry had met with some success, but the appeal of collective farming had barely registered with them. This was not as serious as it might have been, though, as the growth of individualistic and capitalistic practices among the peasantry, which the moves towards co-operation and collectivisation had been designed to counter, turned out to be much less significant than expected. The concessions to the market and capitalism which the Bolsheviks had adopted as means to both political survival and economic development had not resulted in significant increases in either the capitalist tendencies of the peasants, or the marketed surpluses of agricultural products. The chief effect of the move to NEP, for the majority of peasants, had been the easing of the burden placed on them by the state and the cessation of the ruthless means of collection which had been employed during the War Communism period. The overall effect on the peasantry, then, had been to improve their lives sufficiently to undermine the threat of open revolt, but without providing opportunities for more than a tiny minority to rise out of petty-proprietorship into the ranks of the kulaks.

We noted above that many of the aims of NEP bore a close resemblance to the developments which Marx identified as happening in England during the transition from feudalism to capitalism – and which form a large part of the conceptual requirements which Marx identifies as necessary to that transition. In practice, though, the relevant processes (development of a rural proletariat, concentration of ownership, increased production allowing surpluses sufficient to support urbanisation and industrial development etc.) did not achieve really significant development under NEP. The grain harvest in 1927-28 had not quite recovered to its 1913 level, despite a small increase in the sown area.[285] Lower output and higher peasant consumption left less grain for the urban and industrial populations, and less grain for exports, in turn leading to shortages of the required tools and materials with which to modernise both agriculture and industry. Lewin calculated that, by 1928, 5.5 million peasant households (22 per cent) still used wooden ploughs (sokha), half of the harvest was reaped by hand with scythes and sickles and 40 per cent was threshed with flails.[286] This failure to stimulate agricultural modernisation was partly due to the government's unwillingness to see a kulak class develop to a position of influence, and partly because of the circumstances of backwardness and the recent history of chaos and destruction in Russia.

Industry

While peasant unrest had declined significantly, the further aims of the agrarian policies of NEP – to increase production in order to stimulate and to provide for urbanisation and industrialisation – had not been so well met. For light industry, as with agriculture, the Bolsheviks had moved away from the measures of War Communism in 1921, the rebuilding of industry was to take place on a new commercial basis. At this time the majority of industrial workers received their wages in kind,[287] with rations and services – where they were available – mainly free. From August 1921 wages were to be paid in money, though it was not until 1924 that this policy was fully established in practice. Also in August 1921, services ceased to be provided for free, and in November of that year rationing was abolished.

The industrial sector was divided into trusts, controlling various numbers of 'enterprises' (factories, mines etc). Commercial accounting was introduced, with materials and wages having to be paid for from resources generated by sales or loans. Enterprises were to survive or fail on the basis of their commercial viability – profit was to be the aim of all enterprises and the criteria by which success was measured. In December 1921 all industrial enterprises of up to ten employees were de-nationalised, with provision for enterprises of up to 20 workers to be able to apply for de-nationalisation. Enterprises under the ownership of the state and controlled by VSNKh (The Supreme Council of National Economy) were made available for lease to the private sector. By the end of 1922, 10,000 such leases had been granted, usually on contracts of 2 to 5 years, and these enterprises accounted for 33 per cent of Soviet industrial production in 1923-24. The majority of these leases concerned windmills with only one or two employees, but at the end of 1922, 3800 leased enterprises employed 15-20 workers, and a year later 5698 employed an average of 16 workers. While the Bolsheviks retained the 'commanding heights' of industry in state hands,[288] the privatisation of light industry, small-scale manufacture and trade was widespread, with 78 per cent of all retail trade in private hands in 1922-23.[289] Figures for the following year suggest that the private sector accounted for 89.7 per cent of the total output of small-scale industry and handicrafts, and in 1925 84.2 per cent of those employed in such enterprises were private craftsmen, with a further 9.9 per cent working as private employees.[290]

The Bolsheviks soon came to realise that by legalising private trade and permitting private control of small-scale industrial production, they had released forces which would be difficult to control:

> It was assumed that, in a more or less socialist manner, we would exchange on a nation-wide scale the products of state industry for the products of agriculture, and through this product-exchange restore large-scale industry... What happened? What happened was...product-exchange collapsed: it collapsed in the sense that it became purchase-and-sale. The retreat had to continue...product-exchange was a failure, the private market proved stronger than us, and we had instead ordinary purchase and sale, trade.[291]

This flourishing of private trade, though, was short-lived. Even the privatised enterprises were answerable to state organs – usually VSNKh, but sometimes local *sovnarkhozy* or industry specific organs. (In the textile industry, for example, there was never a strong VSNKh influence, and the textile division of VSNKh was abolished in 1927, but the state controlled textile wholesales through the Textile Syndicate.) With the power to hire and fire trust officials, to order the transfer of materials from one industry to another, responsibility for production and disposal plans and for inspections of all aspects of production, VSNKh was, in theory, able to exercise a high degree of administrative control over the trusts and their member enterprises. In practice, though, most trusts behaved as autonomous units in the early stages of NEP, making contracts freely with other trusts, private traders and cooperatives, and making their own arrangements for credit.

From 1923, however, VSNKh began to exercise firm economic control over the largely privatised small-scale industrial sector. While it was difficult for VSNKh to translate formal, administrative control mechanisms into actual, practical influence over small-scale production, the beginnings of recovery in the state-controlled heavy industrial sector provided VSNKh with real economic powers over the privatised workshops and small enterprises. The activities of these small-scale production units became increasingly dependent on the state for supplies of fuel, materials and tools – the power to restrict the flow of such supplies gave VSNKh significant influence over private industry, and similar powers over the flow of manufactured goods provided some measure of control over private trade. From 1923 onwards, the state, through VSNKh, extended its control over the economy, and increased its share of production and trade. Enterprises leased by VSNKh to the private sector saw their share of Soviet industrial production fall from 33 per cent in 1923-24 to 17 per cent in 1928. Between 1922 and 1927 the percentage of retail trade in private hands fell from 78 to 37, and the proportion of private interest in wholesale trade and small-scale industry also dwindled as the twenties wore on.[292]

According to D'Encausse, the state's control of heavy industry and the regulatory framework, of which VSNKh was the centre, allowed the regime to 'restrict the autonomy of the enterprises and to take control once more of the whole industrial sector'.[293] It was the state's practical influence over the supply of and demand for industrial goods which helped to resolve the 'scissors crisis' in 1923-24. Though the government had set up a Prices Committee in 1921, the prices fixed by that body had been systematically ignored by both the state and private sectors. Following the severe famines in 1920 and 1921, the harvests of 1922 and 1923 were relatively high, reaching 90 per cent of their 1913 levels and depressing the price the peasants could obtain for grain. Also, during the famine years the proportion of sown area given to industrial crops fell as the peasants sought to produce food for themselves at the expense of marketable produce. The lack of industrial crops affected many industries with textiles suffering more than most – cotton declined from a sown area of 688,000 hectares in 1913 to just 70,000 in 1922. While agricultural output of that year was at 75 per cent of the 1913 level, the textile industry could manage only 26 per cent of its 1913 output.[294] Shortages of industrial products combined with good harvests in 1922 and 1923 led to soaring prices of industrial goods, relative to agricultural goods. Industrial prices in October 1923 were 276 per cent of their 1913 level, while agricultural produce fetched only 89 per cent of their 1913 equivalent. By restricting credit (thus forcing enterprises to offload their stocks onto the market) and selling manufactured goods at a loss to the peasants, the government managed to close the 'scissors' quickly and effectively. By 1924, agricultural prices had risen slightly to 92 per cent of their 1913 level, with the figure for industrial goods falling significantly to 131 per cent.[295]

Following this success the government began to use its economic strength more and more to implement policies, which, had they remained merely legislative, would have been largely ignored. As the largest purchaser of grain and largest supplier of both the products of heavy industry and the fuel and materials needed by small-scale industrial enterprises, the government could exercise more control over the economy by directly influencing the flow of such goods than by issuing decrees. As the 1920s wore on, the regime used both economic and legal methods to direct the national economy, with the former approach enjoying more success in almost every case. The trend towards greater state control is also apparent in the increasing influence of economic planning during the NEP period. As early as 1922, GOSPLAN – the State Planning Commission – had been set up to 'work out a single, general state economic plan and methods and means of implementing it'.[296] At this time, though, the 'economic plan' was very different from the 'command economy' plans that were introduced from 1927. Under Lenin, the plan was not to be interpreted as a set of orders, instructions or even targets. The plan in this context was a forecast, to be used as a guide for strategic investment decisions. Following Lenin's death, the role of the plan assumed greater importance within the government. Up to 1924, the Communist Party was not even very strongly represented within GOSPLAN. In that year, of the 527 employees of GOSPLAN, only 49 were party members, and 31 of those had no executive responsibility (drivers, typists etc). As Stalin increased his political power in the second half of the decade, with the party apparatus as his power-base, the influence of the party in the state planning organs and the role of the plan in the economy were continually expanded. The Fifteenth Party Congress, in 1926, declared for the 'strengthening of economic hegemony of large-scale socialist industry over the entire economy of the country'[297] and by June 1927 the Council of People's Commissars was calling for 'a united all-union plan which, being the expression of the economic unity of the Soviet Union would facilitate the maximum development of economic regions on the basis of their specialization...and the maximum utilization of their resources for the purpose of industrialisation of the country'.[298] By this time the drive against private trade was already having an effect, and new measures, such as the increases in surcharges for transport of private goods by rail and increased taxes on 'super-profits', were introduced to further discourage the Nepmen. The share of national income in the private sector which had reached a peak of 54.1 per cent in 1925-26 saw a rapid decline as a result of these policies to 27.8 per cent in 1930 and just 9.3 per cent in 1932. This offensive against private trade, together with the formal approval of the first Five-Year Plan in 1929, signalled the end of NEP despite Stalin's claims as late as 1931 that it was still in operation, and despite both private trade and private employment remaining legal until 1930.

The End of the New Economic Policy

Why then was NEP brought to an end less than a decade after its introduction? Lenin had warned, in 1923, that even to 'achieve through NEP the participation of the whole people in cooperatives will require a whole historical epoch'.[299] Tsipko argues that NEP was abandoned because its basis was never really accepted by – or acceptable to – the majority of party members.[300] While Lenin was alive, the unique respect accorded to him as the father of the revolution allowed him to present NEP as an acceptable retreat. With Lenin's death, NEP's days were numbered. Though the debate about the future of NEP was intense following Lenin's death, the chief supporters of NEP – Bukharin and Rykov, who advocated continued steady development and industrialisation within an NEP framework – were undone as much by circumstances as by any latent dislike of the retreat among the party hierarchy, or the party as a whole. Stalin's victory in the struggle to succeed Lenin was largely a measure of his political abilities, but several factors outside the sphere of the intra-party manoeuvring were decisive in the fall of NEP.

Importantly, recovery under NEP had been slower than expected. Agricultural output in 1924 had reached just over half of its 1913 level (51.4 per cent) and, as has been noted above, was still below that even in 1926.[301] The increased freedom given to the peasants under NEP also led to a lower proportion of agricultural products reaching the marketplace, hampering industrial development and holding back urbanisation.[302] The number of blue collar workers – as a proportion of the employed population – declined from 14 per cent in 1913 to 12 per cent in 1928, though white collar workers doubled from 3 per cent to 6 per cent in the same period. Industrial production, measured in roubles, recovered to its 1913 level in 1926, but output of coal, iron-ore, pig-iron, steel and crude petroleum was still some way short of pre-war levels.[303]

> Maurice Dobb suggests that the dilemma facing the Soviet leadership was 'whether priority should be given in the construction programme to heavy industry, which by tackling the crucial bottle-neck would the sooner permit the rate of total construction to be stepped-up, or whether priority should be given to light industry, which would yield its fruit more quickly in a larger supply of consumers' goods, with which to raise the urban standard of life or to tempt more agricultural supplies from the peasantry and expand the trade turnover between town and village'.[304]

Whichever path was chosen, agricultural productivity would need to be increased in order to feed the growing numbers of industrial workers and urban dwellers, and if possible to provide a surplus to be exported in order to purchase much needed plant and machinery. The extent to which this would be possible through the provision of improved implements and more incentives to the peasantry was limited. A move to large-scale agriculture, with modern crop-rotation, an end to strip farming and the modernisation and standardisation of agrarian production relations, permitting mechanisation and efficient labour use, would be necessary if Soviet agricultural production was to improve sufficiently to support further industrial development of any significant degree.

Giving priority to light industry, perhaps within the framework of a continuation of NEP, would result in slower overall development, but would be an essentially conciliatory route – in terms of the relationship between the state and the peasants, and also, to some extent, in terms of the relationship between the Soviet Union and the capitalist powers. The main drawback of this approach was that it could lead to the strengthening of capitalist elements, relying on the kulak class to modernise agriculture and on the Nepmen to handle the complex distribution required by an industrialising society, perhaps leading even to a 'gradual sapping of the socialist key positions that had already been won'.[305]

The alternative to a kulak-led modernisation of agriculture was a move to modern, large-scale cultivation directed by the state. This approach would necessarily be more confrontational than that outlined above, with not just the kulaks, but also the mass of middle-peasant petty-proprietors facing the confiscation of land and implements they held to be their own.

Stalin's early comments on collectivisation urged an end to NEP, but proposed moderate methods and a gradual solution to the problem of the slow rate of agricultural development and its detrimental effect on industrialisation:

What is the way out? The way out is to turn the small and scattered peasant farms into large united farms based on cultivation of the land in common, to go over to collective cultivation of the land on the basis of a new, higher technique. The way out is to unite the small and dwarf peasant farms gradually but surely, not by pressure but by example and persuasion, into large farms based on common, co-operative, collective cultivation of the land...There is no other way out.[306]

Note that again we see the leadership of the socialist regime calling for a move to large-scale agriculture; for the transformation of scattered pygmy property into concentrated property; for one of the processes which Marx identifies as crucial to the transition from feudalism to capitalism.

3.3 Stalin – Collectivisation and the Five-Year Plans

The Fifteenth Party Congress (December 1927), at which Stalin made this speech, resolved to undertake the collectivisation of Russian agriculture as a 10 to 15-year process. At the Congress the following year, the first Five-Year Plan was approved including a resolution to collectivise 26 million hectares by the end of the plan, to account for 15 per cent of agricultural output. It soon became apparent, though, that 'example and persuasion' were inappropriate means for getting the peasants into collectives in sufficient numbers. NEP had won valuable breathing space for the regime against the threat of peasant insurrection and, having re-grouped, the government began to display an air of confidence in its agrarian policies. In May 1929 Stalin announced that, in order to increase the rate of development, the government would launch a campaign to collectivise the peasantry – the majority of the peasantry, rather than the 15 per cent indicated in the plan, and with 'immediate effect', rather than within the 5 years of the plan. During this time, the methods employed by the state in dealings with the peasantry had reverted to the ruthlessness of the War Communism period. In January and February 1928, following reports of good harvests in the Urals and in west Siberia, but with low procurement rates in those areas, Stalin personally oversaw the forcible seizure of stocks of grain by police and party officials.[307] This action was repeated in 1929 and, known as the 'Urals-Siberian method', became commonplace in the following years.

What, then, was behind this change of policy, from gradual collectivisation on the basis of persuasion and incentives to accelerated collectivisation with little regard for the views of the peasants? Given that NEP was always regarded as a retreat by the Bolsheviks, it was perhaps predictable that the offensive against peasant individualism would be resumed as soon as the government felt confident enough to do so. There were, though, other factors which may be regarded as contributing to the drive to all out collectivisation.

First, the realisation that steady collectivisation, by persuasion, was unlikely to gain many recruits while the option of petty-proprietorship remained, and that it would be difficult to sustain significant levels of collectivised farming alongside a private sector.

Second, the acceptance, by party theoreticians in the mid-1920s, that capitalism in the West had temporarily stabilised and that the Soviets could face an extended period of isolation. In 1925 Stalin suggested that they would have to wait at least 20 years before they could expect any external assistance.[308] Given such a timescale the USSR's position looked more precarious, and the prospect of at least 2 more decades of the growth in size and influence of the kulak class (already perceived to be much greater than was actually the case) added potential internal threats to the regime to concern over possible hostilities from abroad.

The importance of the perceived external threat should not be underestimated. N. Shmelev has argued that it is a mistake to justify Stalin's policies with reference to the threat of war, as the Nazi's were an insignificant force in the late 1920s. Yet the capitalist powers which Stalin saw as 'encircling' the USSR had taken military action against the revolutionary regime before and many in Russia feared that they would do so again. The year 1924 had been called the 'year of recognition' due to the number of Western powers that established diplomatic relations with the Soviet Union at that time. In 1927 Britain, France, Canada, Poland and others broke off such relations and the Politburo 'declared that Poland and France, supported by the League [of Nations] and egged on by British Conservatives, were about to invade the USSR'.[309] In such an atmosphere, effective military development assumed great importance and this would only be possible with a rate of industrial development unobtainable without the rapid modernisation of agriculture.

The end of the civil war had been the first opportunity for the Bolsheviks to introduce a set of peacetime policies, yet NEP was as much a reaction to the unfavourable circumstances of 1921 as War Communism had been to those of 1917-18. The most pressing need in 1921 had been to appease the peasantry, to secure the regime against potentially catastrophic unrest, and NEP was undoubtedly successful in this respect. Though the concessions to the peasantry were regarded as a partial 'retreat' to capitalism, the Bolsheviks could see some positive aspects in this new direction. Aware that their revolution had been 'premature' in historical materialist terms, but also of the opinion that the pre-revolutionary regime had been of an essentially capitalist nature, the Bolsheviks considered capitalist relations of production to be well suited to further development of the productive forces at the then existing level. By introducing elements of capitalism to Soviet society (primarily for reasons of political survival) they could expect swift recovery from the destruction and chaos of the war years. Accompanying this expectation, however, was the fear that NEP would result in a new danger through the strengthening of the capitalistic kulak class, and their counterparts in trade, the Nepmen. Neither the expectations concerning the speed of economic development or the fears of increasing capitalist tendencies among the peasants materialised to a significant extent. (Though the size and influence of the kulak class was persistently over-estimated and overstated by the regime.) I have argued that these policies, had they been successful, would have set in motion some of the processes which Marx identifies as part of the transition from feudalism to capitalism. This is also the case with the policies which replaced NEP in the late 1920s. The move towards collectivisation was largely motivated by the awareness that the introduction of large-scale, modern agriculture was absolutely crucial to the further development of industry – to the further development of the productive forces in the Soviet Union. Such development was an obvious objective for the Soviet leadership, but it assumed greater importance and urgency with the realisation, towards the end of the decade, that revolutions in the West were unlikely to occur in the near future. Given the potential difficulties involved in a gradualist approach to collectivisation, and given the regime's confidence in its ability to impose unpopular measures on the peasantry, policies of immediate collectivisation and rapid development of heavy industry were adopted.

In terms of these goals, the policies met with some success. We noted in Chapter 1.6 that agricultural productivity in Russia in 1913 was lower than that in England in 1600. By 1939, after only 22 years of Soviet rule – and with nearly 90 per cent of peasant households collectivised – productivity had reached an equivalent of mid-nineteenth century Britain.[310] Making up 250 years of progress in a few decades was obviously helped by the fact that the Soviets didn't have to keep waiting for technological developments to be invented, or to waste years and decades finding out that a particular development was actually a dead-end. Nevertheless, the advances were dramatic. Collectivisation and mechanisation of agriculture enabled rapid urbanisation, with the urban population more than doubling from 26 million in 1926 to 56 million in 1939, though even the latter figure accounted for only 34 per cent of the population[311] – a figure surpassed in Britain in the early nineteenth century. Urbanisation wasn't a goal in itself, but was a necessary process if the industrialisation targets of the Five-Year Plans were to be met. The targets under Stalin were hugely ambitious – bearing little resemblance to what was actually possible and contributing to the increasing brutality of the regime, already in overdrive as a result of Stalin's paranoia and the perceived encirclement of the USSR by capitalist powers. As with earlier periods, the reality of Soviet development bore little resemblance to socialist ambitions, or even to the Soviets' own blueprint: As Mark Sandle notes, 'One of the enduring paradoxes of this period was the contrast between the legal structure of authority and the practice of the system.'[312] By the late 1930s the threat of war was becoming ever more real and the third Five-Year Plan was recast to reflect the new priorities. The Soviet Union would be a formidable force in the Second World War – in stark contrast to the shambolic failure of Imperial Russia in the First. Despite the devastation wreaked by intense combat on Soviet territory, and the millions killed and maimed in the war, the Soviet industrial machine took up in 1945 where it had left off in 1941 and the fourth Five-Year Plan promised great strides by 1950. Respite from the relentless drive for ever more industrial might, requiring ever increasing output by the state farms, was only to come with Stalin's death in 1953. After nearly 3 decades in power it was 3 years before the regime publicly acknowledged even a limited set of his crimes against the people. The process of de-Stalinisation had been going on quietly since his death, but such was the paranoia of the time the manoeuvring had to be taken slowly with even those at the very top of the party and state machinery in precarious positions as the post-Stalin regime took shape.

3.4 The USSR After Stalin

Although the Soviet Union underwent significant changes in the aftermath of Stalin's death, there was also a degree of continuity. While political, social and cultural life was overhauled in the process of de-Stalinisation, the economy experienced less significant change. Noises were made about shifting the focus from heavy industry to consumer goods, but even by 1985 the production of consumer goods had increased by a smaller margin since 1955 than the production of producers' goods.[313] The Soviet system had proved adequate for importing technology and developing industry from pre-capitalist levels up to the level commensurate with early capitalism, but there came a point when it could not develop the productive forces any further – even with the benefits of technological advances from the West it was hopelessly ill-suited to further development.

One of the earliest problems addressed by both Malenkov and Khrushchev in the mid-1950s was that of the supply of labour in the agricultural sector – and this remained a major thorn in Gorbachev's side in the 1980s, with the agricultural sector still accounting for over 7 per cent of the workforce. By this point it was becoming clear that the Soviet system was hindering further development. The frustration with the system was evident in the comments of an anonymous official of *Agroprom* in a 1986 issue of *Novyi Mir (New World)*: 'With one hand we write good decrees, promising the village scope for decision, fresh air, stimuli, while with the other hand we tear them to shreds.' The same edition printed an observation from A. Shvelyany that today 'in many places is like 1952, 1962, 1972 and 1982...first the plan, then the plan-task, then the first supplementary plan, then the second...'[314]

Conventional wisdom often sees the succession of Gorbachev – at 54 the youngest member of a Politburo dominated by septuagenarians – as a turning point in Soviet history. As the system crumbled, the story goes, the ageing leadership crumbled with it until the young reformer burst onto the scene. But reform had been in the air for some years before Gorbachev's appointment, partly due to increasing international interactions under Brezhnev – by 1980 the Soviet Union had diplomatic relations with 139 countries and trade relations with 145, compared to 79 and 45 respectively a few decades earlier.[315] The difference, in Ronald Suny's words, was that before Gorbachev the leadership's idea of reform 'was to improve the system without seriously altering its basic contours'. Brezhnev's successor, Yuri Andropov, had spent time as ambassador to Hungary in the 1950s, and although he'd been instrumental in the brutal put down of the 1956 uprising, he'd also seen how a degree of economic liberalism could work within the command economy. On his succession in 1982 he began to promote younger, reforming members through the party ranks. Andropov died only 14 months into his leadership and his party reforms couldn't prevent the accession of the geriatric Brezhnevite Konstantin Chernenko – whose reign was even briefer than Andropov's. On Chernenko's death in 1985 the old guard could resist no more and Gorbachev was nominated by the elder statesman of the Politburo, Gromyko, who referred to the new leader as 'a man with a nice smile, but iron teeth'.[316]

Gorbachev introduced two new concepts to Soviet political life – *Glasnost* (transparency) and *Perestroika* (restructuring). The Soviet system had become almost mummified by inertia. Misinformation was commonplace, to the extent that no one expected statistics to bear any relationship to reality. The party apparatus was such that people had no choice but to act in the interests of their own self-preservation – a situation which stifled innovation and progress. At the Twenty-Seventh Party Congress in 1986 Boris Yeltsin (then head of the CPSU organisation in Moscow) denounced 'time-servers in possession of Party cards'.[317] The political organisation and political culture of the USSR had stagnated since the upheavals of de-Stalinisation and though the economy had lumbered on, the system had become unreformable.

Still though, Gorbachev thought the system could be reformed – at no point was his aim the end of the Soviet Union. The dynamic at work in the USSR after de-Stalinisation – if dynamic isn't too strong a word for it – was that the further development of the forces of production could not take place within the existing economic structure. But, as with the transition to capitalism elsewhere, those involved could not see this dynamic – they were too close to the action. No one who was anyone seriously thought that capitalism was the answer to Soviet stagnation. They tried any number of experiments, and eventually, with Gorbachev and then Yeltsin rising to prominence, the experiments gathered a momentum of their own and the writing was on the wall for the Soviet system. The political, social and cultural life of Russia was about to catch up with the level of technological development they had reached decades earlier – capitalism was just around the corner.

In 1986 the slow and secretive response to the Chernobyl disaster highlighted the problems of the political system and the devastation caused by the collapse in world oil prices illustrated the problems of the monolithic command economy. Gorbachev and Yeltsin had promoted the concept of more or less gradual reform, within the parameters of the Soviet system, but the air of reform they unleashed was unstoppable because the development of the productive forces had reached a level where further development would require capitalist relations of production. The proliferation of consumer society in the West helped to create a desire for further and faster development among the Soviet citizenry, as well as demands for political liberation, religious freedom and national self-determination. But the Soviet system was inflexible – it could not be reformed, it had to be replaced. By January 1987 Gorbachev told the central committee that retreat was impossible as there was nowhere left to retreat to. A tipping point had been reached. The end of the Soviet experiment was in sight. At last the political system would give way to the march of progress. Following extensive strikes by miners in Siberia and the Ukraine in 1989 the Supreme Soviet finally recognised the right to strike. After Lithuania and Estonia declared themselves sovereign republics in May of the same year Moscow recognised their right to do so. The border between Hungary and Austria came down in the same month. Three months later Solidarity swept the Polish elections and by November the fall of the Berlin Wall symbolised the end of the Eastern Bloc and the decline of Soviet influence. Events overtook the leadership. Hardline party traditionalists failed to oust Gorbachev in an unsuccessful coup in August 1991. Before the year ended the Soviet Union was voted out of existence by the Supreme Soviet, to be replaced by the Commonwealth of Independent States. The experiment was over, and so was the bourgeois revolution that no one had noticed was under way. Capitalism had arrived in Russia.

Conclusions

So what have we learnt? Or unlearnt as the case may be... We've learnt that we can dismiss the death toll hysteria created by those trying to pin mass murder on the left, so that having Hitler on their side of the spectrum doesn't seem so bad. We can dismiss this not only because the numbers are so absurd, but more importantly because Stalin, Pol Pot and the rest really aren't anything to do with the left.

With that nonsense out of the way, we can look at the more constructive lessons we can draw from Marx's work. Obviously a central aim of this work has been to present a new interpretation of the place of the Soviet Union in the history of global development. In order to do this we've looked at Marx's approach to historical change and the way in which he categorises societies and the way they transition from one economic structure to another. It's important to note that this approach is not meant to *replace* other explanations of historical events, but largely to *complement* them. To say that the English civil war, for example, was a political and social reflection of underlying economic changes still allows room for us to accept detailed explanations focused on the actions and motives of the main protagonists. Placing such events within a theory of development doesn't require us to explain every battle or instance of political skulduggery with reference to that theory. What it says, rather, is that however events turned out, behind the scenes the march of technological progress was not going to be subverted indefinitely. Had Prince Rupert not lost his head at the Battle of Edgehill on a Thursday afternoon in 1642, and had he instead routed the Parliamentary forces, capitalism would still have developed in England. It may have taken longer, it may have taken a different form, but it was coming – and by the same token, one day, it's going.

By letting go of the influence of Bolshevik leaders on Marx's work, and by focusing on his theory of history rather than his political polemics or detailed economic analysis I have argued that the Soviet Union (together with the last half century of Tsarist rule) represents – in Marx's terms – the essential processes of Russia's bourgeois revolution – of Russia's transition from feudalism to capitalism. Hopefully, this explanation can serve not only to help us to understand Russian and Soviet history better than we otherwise would, but also to see the value of viewing historical change from this perspective.

Using the framework provided by Marx, we can see that capitalism is running out of steam. For a couple of centuries it has provided the means to produce more and better and faster. But the level of technological development it has delivered means that we have now entered a post-scarcity world. Twenty thousand people starve to death every day. Not because we don't have the food to feed them – but because our current economic and social mechanisms don't allow us to deliver that food to them. Although there is room within capitalism for a level of philanthropy, as a system it is fundamentally incapable of solving this problem. Capitalism has never worked on supply and demand – it works on supply and *demand-plus-ability-to-pay*. What we need now is a system that can accommodate progress as a function of distribution and increasing equality, not just as the production of ever more stuff for people who already have too much, while others perish for the lack of the means of survival. The version of Marx's approach I have presented here not only indicates where we need to go, but also how we need to get there. We are not going to progress past capitalism by seizing the means of production in armed conflict. We don't have the guns, and as long as the right-wing media is most people's interface with the political world we don't have the numbers either. But look at the lessons we've learnt. The English bourgeois revolution wasn't won on the battlefields of the civil wars – it was won in the workshops of inventors and in the imagination of forward-thinking individuals who could see a better way of doing things. The challenges to capitalism will come from new approaches to the relationships between work and leisure, between work and reward, between possession and ownership and between private property and public value. It's important to note that this is not what Marxists have traditionally referred to as *reformism*. This isn't advocating an attempt to bring out the potential for capitalism to be less iniquitous. This is advocating an overthrow of capitalism by changing the economic structure in the only way it ever really changes – slowly, and in response to changing circumstances, by utilising technological developments created within the existing system.

Appendix – Death Toll Olympics

There seems to be a recent trend from certain right-leaning commentators to forego all the boring leg-work and the pouring over historical documents in favour of a new statistical technique whereby the number of deaths attributable to communism is arrived at by plucking a number from the air at random and multiplying it by 10 million. Dominic Sandbrook is so adept at this technique he can perform it numerous times in the space of a single article for the Daily Mail where Mao's death toll oscillates by several millions more than once and Pol Pot's increases by 20 per cent over the space of a few dozen lines.[318] In the end, though, Sandbrook's largest guesses total a fairly conservative 60 million between Stalin, Mao and Pol Pot. Jordan Peterson is less restrained, bouncing from 30 million Soviet deaths here to 60 million there, then slipping 100 million in for Mao like he's tipping a waiter – 'it's ok son, you've earned it'.[319]

The reason for all of this number-wanging is clear. With the death count of the holocaust fixed (correctly) in the public imagination at around 6 million, all kinds of means are being employed to relegate this to something less than the uniquely monstrous episode that it was in an attempt to demonstrate that the (regimes they would like us to think of as) far-left were just as bad as the far-right. (Remember that whenever a commentator deliberately exaggerates the death toll of communism for this purpose, what they're actually doing is minimising the horrors of the holocaust. It's not a good look. The point of this tactic is to shut down debate – to pre-empt any reasonable discussion of left-wing policies by hysterically screeching about 100 million deaths.) Counting deaths by the million isn't actually the best way to evaluate totalitarian regimes, or to locate our moral compass on today's political landscape. The whole process of counting deaths and deciding which are to be tallied against one dictator or another is pretty distasteful, but if the right are going to lie about it, then they do need to be corrected.

There is no doubt that regimes identifying as socialist spent a lot of the twentieth century oppressing sizeable chunks of their populations, and the death toll is significant. The nature of the Soviet regime makes any kind of statistical work notoriously difficult, and estimates within realistic ranges are the best we can hope for. The broad academic consensus puts the death toll under Stalin at between 6 and 9 million[320] over 29 years with some historians maintaining figures up to 15 million, though admittedly through processes of speculative interpolation.[321]

The holocaust was carried out in accordance with an ideologically driven plan, and resulted in the systematic murder of 6 million people, including two-thirds of Europe's Jewish population in little more than a decade. The death count under Stalin – remember, we are *not* engaged in any attempt at justification here, we are providing context and restoring accuracy to an issue much abused by the populist right – the death toll under Stalin runs to around 9 million over nearly 3 decades *if* we include victims of persecution, deaths in labour camps *and* deaths caused by famine and disease as a result of negligence, ill-advised policies and deliberate withholding of supplies. But if we're going to count all those deaths, then Hitler's count is going to need revising upwards to include far more casualties than the 6 million holocaust victims. In fact, if we're going to include deaths caused by starvation due to misallocation of resources, we need to decide what to do with the 7 million people who starve to death every year under global capitalism. As I stated above, I don't want to give the impression that I'm defending Stalin's monstrous policies, or that I think comparing death tolls has any benefit. If anything, I'm trying to show that both the incomplete historical record and the lack of consensus on how to approach which deaths to include make the process as impossible as it is futile. Plucking figures out of the air and multiplying them by 10 million for the purpose of making Hitler seem less of a psychopath seems to me to be an extreme way to approach the issue. Let's have more historical accuracy and less of the playing-down of Nazi atrocities.

Notes

1 Here we will use the term *Marxian* to refer to the ideas of Marx, as opposed to *Marxist* which often refers to the ideas of later theorists who may or may not base their work on that of Marx. The term *Marxist* is also in danger of becoming meaningless as it's currently most often used by right-wing commentators to refer to anything or any person of which they disapprove.

2 There is a possible exception to this statement, but it would only come into play following a specified chain of events, which didn't materialise. This is covered in Chapter 1.4.

3 This isn't hyperbole – Jordan Peterson actually claims that any move towards equality of outcome is 'detestable and dangerous beyond belief' because it's the slippery slope towards the gulags. https://www.youtube.com/watch?v=3wj48ACMWeI&t=17m05s

4 The nonsense of the inflated death count ought to have no place in a serious work but such is its currency in what passes for current political debate, I have added an appendix to this work to address that issue.

5 Though they were not always as relentlessly miserable as Cold War propaganda would have us believe.

6 There are people out there who think that because Hitler's Nazis called themselves *National Socialists* that they were a socialist party and therefore a phenomenon that the left needs to own or explain or apologise for. To be blunt, those people have a lot of reading to do before they're ready for the present discussion. We won't be addressing their complaints here.

7 John Pilger in the *New Statesman*, 17 April 2000. https://www.newstatesman.com/politics/politics/2014/04/how-thatcher-gave-pol-pot-hand

8   East Germany, Poland, Hungary, Bulgaria, Romania, Yugoslavia, Czechoslovakia, Albania.

9   China, North Korea, Vietnam, Laos, Cuba, Nicaragua etc.

10   LENIN, V.I. *Collected Works* Vol. 25. Lawrence and Wishart, 1962, p69.

11   MARX, K. 'Results of the Direct Process of Production'. See MARX, K *and* ENGELS,F. *Collected Works*. Lawrence and Wishart, 1975. Vol. XXXIV, p399. (Henceforth *MECW*)

12   MARX, K *and* ENGELS,F. *Collected Works*. Lawrence and Wishart, 1975. Vol. V, p49.

13   This does not entail, of course, that there are no other preconditions for the establishment of communism.

14   This statement is so uncontroversial that it should need no supporting evidence, but should you require any, see Chapter 3.1.

15   Zasulich (1849-1919) a socialist revolutionary in exile in Geneva, later co-founder of *Iskra* and a member of the Menshevik faction of the RSDLP.

16   Zasulich to Marx 16/2/1881. See SHANIN,T. (ed.) *Late Marx and the Russian Road*. Routledge, 1984, p99.

17   Marx to Zasulich 8/3/1881. See MARX,K and ENGELS,F. *Collected Works Vol. XXIV*. Lawrence and Wishart, 1975, p370.

18   MARX, K and ENGELS,F. *Collected Works* Vol. XXIV Lawrence and Wishart, 1975, p426.

19   LENIN, V.I. *Collected Works* Vol X, Lawrence and Wishart, 1962, p333-4. (From 'Report on the Unity Congress of the RSDLP – A Letter to the St Petersburg Workers'. May/June 1906.)

20   Quoted in KNEI-PAZ,R. *The Social and Political Thought of Leon Trotsky*. Oxford University Press, 1978, p140. (From 'Results and Prospects'.)

21   Some of the terms used in Historical Materialism are also used in wider, general conversation and in such cases

the meaning is rarely the same. Terms such as *class* and *revolution* have particular, tightly defined meanings in Historical Materialism. Others, such as *exploitation* or *bourgeois*, may come with considerable baggage in general usage, but here should be considered as descriptive terms of particular phenomena, as defined below.

22 Although we may sometimes employ the legal terminology of 'ownership', this should always be taken to mean 'effective control', which is often, but not always, the same as ownership. For extensive justification of this decision, see Cohen, G.A. *Karl Marx's Theory of History – A Defence* Princeton University Press, 1976. Chapter VIII.

23 COHEN, G.A. (1976), p134.

24 COHEN, G.A. (1976), p135.

25 COHEN, G.A. Functional Explanation: Reply to Elster. *Political Studies* Vol.XXVIII, No.1. 1980, p129.

26 MARX, K. *Capital I*. Lawrence and Wishart, 1954, p714.

27 MARX, K. *Deutsche-Brüsseler-Zeitung* No. 92, 18 November 1847. (MARX, K and ENGELS, F. *Collected Works* Vol. VI, p319.)

28 There's no suggestion that urbanisation or industrialisation were conscious aims of anyone at the time. But they are the processes that developed, and they could not have done so on the back of sixteenth-century outputs.

29 The total sown area of arable land in England in 1800 was 11.5m acres. See OVERTON,M. *Agricultural Revolution in England – The Transformation of the Agrarian Economy 1500-1850*. Cambridge University Press, 1996, p126.

30 MARX, K. *Capital I*, p724.

31 MARX, K. *Capital I*, p714.

32 For further discussion of the transition from feudalism to capitalism in England, see my *After Capitalism*.

33 MARX, K. *Capital I*, Chapter 28.

34 MARX, K. *Deutsche-Brüsseler-Zeitung* No. 92, November 18

1847. (MARX, K and ENGELS,F. *Collected Works* Vol. VI, p 319.)

35 See Chapter 3.1.

36 NOVE, A. *Studies in Economics and Russia.* Macmillan, 1990, p43.

37 1905 Statistical Yearbook. See PUSHKAREV, S. *The Emergence of Modern Russia 1801-1917.* Pica Pica Press, 1985, p278.

38 EDELMAN, R. *Gentry Politics on the Eve of the Russian Revolution.* New Brunswick: Rutgers University Press, 1980, p15.

39 KLEBNIKOV, P.G. *Agricultural Development in Russia, 1906-17: Land Reform, Social Agronomy and Cooperation.* 1991. p 352 (PhD Dissertation, at http://etheses.lse.ac.uk/1141/1/U048311.pdf), and OVERTON,M. *Agricultural Revolution in England – The Transformation of the Agrarian Economy 1500-1850.* Cambridge University Press, 1996, p77.

40 WALKIN, J. *The Rise of Democracy in Pre-Revolutionary Russia.* Thames and Hudson, 1963, p.107-8.

41 See WARD, C. *Stalin's Russia* (2nd ed.) Arnold, 1999, p39.

42 COHEN, G.A. Functional Explanation: Reply to Elster. *Political Studies* Vol.XXVIII, No.1. 1980, p129.

43 That's not to say that historical materialists have neglected to discuss the transitional structure at all, but coverage has been largely by historians discussing the transition from feudalism to capitalism, rather than the nature of the concept of transitional structures.

44 THOMPSON, E.P. *The Making of the English Working Class.* Penguin, 1968, p85.

45 THOMPSON, E.P. (1968), p10.

46 From ELSTER, J. *Making Sense of Marx.* Cambridge University Press, 1985, p 345-6.

47 ELSTER, J. (1985), p346.

48 From COHEN, G.A. (1978), p76.

49   COHEN, G.A. (1976), p76.

50   MARX, K. *The Poverty of Philosophy* Moscow: Progress Publishers, 1975, p160.

51   See ELSTER, J. (1985), p346.

52   POULANTZAS, N. *Classes in Contemporary Capitalism. New Left Books*, 1975. p 14.

53   Nor does historical materialism require this view of class.

54   The central point here is that it is the features of the individual's class location which make the revolutionary option a rational one.

55   MARX, K. *Capital I*, p672.

56   MARX, K. *Capital I*, p676.

57   MARX, K. *Capital I*, p674.

58   MARX, K. *Capital I*, p668.

59   ELSTER, J. (1985), p322.

60   COHEN, G.A. (1978), p73.

61   COHEN, G.A. (1978), p72.

62   COHEN, G.A. (1978), p73.

63   MARX, K. *Grundrisse*. Penguin, 1973, p 510.

64   COHEN, G.A. (1978), p69.

65   Under feudalism, of course, subordination plays a direct role in identifying class relations. The subordination of the serf derives directly from his structural conditions – he is only partly in control of his labour power and is subordinated to the feudal lord by virtue of the latter's partial ownership of that labour power.

66   See the section on the mode of exploitation under capitalism in Chapter 2.3.

67   COHEN, G.A. (1978), p145. The term 'scientific' should here be taken in its broadest sense.

68   WRIGHT, E.O. What is Middle About the Middle Class? In ROEMER, J. (ed) *Analytical Marxism*. Cambridge University Press, 1986.

69   WRIGHT, E.O. *Class, Crisis and the State*. New Left Books,

1978, p71, fn.

70 POULANTZAS, N. *Classes in Contemporary Capitalism.* New Left Books, 1975, p 180. Poulantzas is here concerned only with managers who directly control capital assets. He regards technical experts – engineers, architects etc – as a fraction of the 'new petty-bourgeoisie'.

71 This is true *by definition* since their control is a feature of their employment, and their powers of control would be withdrawn upon leaving that employment. Self-employed technocrats who sell not their labour power, but the product of their labour, may exercise a similar degree of control over means of production, but their control is not a feature of their employment (since they are not employed), but of their operations in the competitive market. Those who 'work' but who also engage in commercial activity in their own right should not be classified as members of the 'technocracy', but as members of the petty-bourgeoisie.

72 ELSTER, J. in ROEMER,J. (ed.) (1986), p143.

73 ROEMER, J. New Directions in the Marxian Theory of Exploitation and Class. *Politics and Society,* vol.11, no. 3, 1982, p253-87.

74 HODGES, D. The Intermediate Classes in Marxian Theory. *Social Research,* 23, 1961.

75 Here, behavioural considerations are invoked as mediating criteria in the determination of class locations. The petty-bourgeois are defined in terms of their control over productive forces, while that control is measured by reference to the behaviour which is necessitated by the extent and nature of that control. 'Necessary behaviour' is favoured over actual behaviour because it serves as a more suitable indicator of structural conditions. Many bourgeois also work – they are bourgeois because their ownership of productive assets is such that they could live without working.

76 MARX, K. *Preface and Introduction to A Contribution to the Critique of Political Economy.* (1859). Peking: Foreign Languages Press, 1976, p3.

77 MARX, K. (1976), p68.

78 VINOGRADOFF, P. *Villainage in England – Essays in English Mediaeval History.* Oxford University Press,1968, p83.

79 COHEN, G.A, p181.

80 MARX, K *Capital I*, p166. Note that ownership of some means of production is not, strictly speaking, incompatible with proletarian status. The proletarian differs from the serf, in this context, in that the former does not possess *sufficient* means of production to escape the economic compulsion to sell his labour power to another.

81 While some degree of wage labour is not always incompatible with serf-status, the freedom of the serf in this respect is considerably less than that enjoyed by true proletarians. (See below for further discussion.)

82 MARX, K *Capital I*, p165.

83 For example, Ranulf Glanville De Legibus et consuetudinibus regni Angliae, Henry de Bracton De Legibus et consuetudinibus Angliae. See VINOGRADOFF,P. (1968), p130-5 and KOSMINSKY,E.A. *Studies in the Agrarian History of England in the Thirteenth Century.* Oxford: Basil Blackwell,1956, p330.

84 Glanville, See VINOGRADOFF,P. (1968), p85.

85 *Dialogus de Scaccario ii.* See VINOGRADOFF,P. (1968), p44.

86 KOSMINSKY, E.A. (1956), p337.

87 VINOGRADOFF, P. (1968), p85.

88 VINOGRADOFF, P. (1968), p151.

89 MARX, K. *Capital III*, p790.

90 VINOGRADOFF, P. (1968), p166.

91 Glanville See VIOGRADOFF, P. (1968), p165.

92 KOSMINSKY, E.A. op. cit., p337. Kosminsky argues that the state gave protection in order to continue to collect taxes

from the villein population.

93 COHEN, G.A. op. cit., p82.

94 *Capital III*, p790-1.

95 HOBSBAWM, E.J., in editor's introduction to MARX, K. *Pre-Capitalist Economic Formations.* Lawrence and Wishart, 1964, p42.

96 HILTON, R.H. (ed.) *The Transition from Feudalism to Capitalism.* New Left Books, 1976, p14.

97 HILTON, R.H. (1976), p14.

98 COHEN, G.A. (1975), p84.

99 VINOGRADOFF, P. (1968), p166-7.

100 VINOGRADOFF, P. (1968), p83.

101 KOSMINSKY, E.A. (1956), p333-4.

102 KOSMINSKY, E.A. (1956), p294.

103 KOSMINSKY, E.A. (1956), p301.

104 KOSMINSKY, E.A. (1956), p206 and p90.

105 KOSMINSKY, E.A. (1956), p293.

106 KOSMINSKY, E.A. (1956), p202.

107 COHEN, G.A. (1978), p79-84. Cohen usefully distinguishes between the different usages of the phrase 'mode of production' in Marx's writings. He identifies the *'material mode'* which relates to 'the way men work with productive forces', the *'social mode'* which covers the purpose of production, the mode of exploitation and the form of surplus labour, and the *'mixed mode'* which denotes the 'entire technical and social configuration'. Here the phrase 'mode of production' will, unless otherwise stated, refer to the purpose of production. The 'material mode' and the 'mixed (or general) mode' will be referred to as such. The mode of exploitation has been discussed above. Comment on Cohen's treatment of the form of surplus labour is given below.

108 MARX, K. *Capital I,* p151.

109 MARX, K. *Capital I,* p226.

110 SWEEZY, P. in HILTON, R.H. (1976), p35.

111 See PROCACCI, G. In HILTON,R.H. (1976), p132.

112 MARX, K. *Capital II*, p36.

113 MARX, K. *Capital II*, p36.

114 COHEN, G.A. (1978), p78-9.

115 MARX, K. *Capital II* (1956), p123.

116 And in relation to whole economies.

117 COHEN, G.A. (1978), p181-2.

118 SWEEZY, P. in HILTON, R.H. (1976), p49.

119 HOBSBAWM, E.J. Pre-capitalist Modes of Production in HILTON, R.H. (1976), p46.

120 DOBB, M. in HILTON,R.H. (1976), p58. See also TAKAHASHI, K, p69.

121 Functional explanation is a form of causal explanation and should not be confused with functionalism.

122 COHEN, G.A. (1978), p134.

123 COHEN, G.A. (1978), p135.

124 RIGBY, S.H. Marxism *and History – A Critical Introduction*. Manchester University Press, 1987, p118.

125 RIGBY,S.H (1987), p124-5.

126 MARX, K. *Capital I*, p235 & 486.

127 RIGBY, S.H. (1987), p124.

128 MARX, K. (1976), p3.

129 COHEN, G.A. (1978), p142.

130 COHEN, G.A. (1978), p155.

131 COHEN, G.A. (1978), p135.

132 COHEN, G.A. (1978), p134.

133 COHEN, G.A. Functional Explanation: Reply to Elster. *Political Studies* Vol.XXVIII, No.1. 1980, p129.

134 COHEN, G.A. (1978), p160.

135 COHEN, G.A. (1978), p161.

136 COHEN, G.A. (1978), p161.

137 COHEN, G.A. (1978), p159.

138 RIGBY, S H. (1987), p299.

139 RIGBY, S H. (1987), p97.

140 RIGBY, S H. (1987), p113.

141 COHEN, G.A. (1978), p98.

142 RIGBY, S.H. (1987), p113.

143 MARX, K. (1976), p2-3.

144 MARX, K *Capital I,* p671.

145 COHEN, G.A. (1978), p177.

146 MARX, K *Capital I,* p669.

147 COHEN, G.A. Reply to Elster on 'Marxism, Functionalism and Game Theory'. In CALLINICOS,A.(ed.) Marxist Theory. Oxford University Press, 1989, p96.

148 COHEN, G.A. (1980), p131.

149 COHEN, G.A. (1980), p131.

150 COHEN, G.A. (1976), p95.

151 COHEN, G.A. (1989), p98.

152 COHEN, G.A. (1980), p131.

153 ELSTER, J. In CALLINICOS,A.(ed.) *Marxist Theory.* Oxford University Press, 1989, p65.

154 COHEN, G.A. (1980), p131.

155 The fact that large-scale production is a profit-maximising strategy is entailed by the premise of the functional fact (that large-scale production reduces costs) and the uncontroversial notion that reduced costs increase profits.

156 COHEN, G.A. (1978), p287.

157 It is hoped that the argument which Cohen mounts against Hempel (see *KMTH*, p273) is not applicable to this generalisation for this reason: Hempel's approach, according to Cohen, concerns conditions which *must* be satisfied in order for a system to survive. The generalisation given here refers to conditions which are more survival-promoting than other viable alternatives. The difference between these two types of condition is sufficient to make the given criticism applicable to one approach and not the other.

158 Cohen lists four types of elaboration which are concerned with how functional-explanatory phenomena may arise. (Purposive, Darwinian, Lamarkian and self-deception, which is a special case of the purposive type.) He adds that the list is not exhaustive and that those given may be combined in a single explanation.

159 It has been argued above that the period in which new economic structures arise is of crucial importance to Marx's theory of history, and to historical understanding generally. But what is important to the concept of functional explanation is not how they arose but why they emerged victorious from the era of social revolution. Indeed, it has been suggested that the functional-explanatory primacy of the forces is at its weakest point *during* the era of social revolution. When Cohen states that 'new relations come into being' because they are apt to develop the forces (*KMTH*, p161) it would be more plausible to make the claim that they *come to dominate the economic structure* because they are apt to develop the forces.

160 MARX, K. *Capital I*, p668.

161 MARX, K. *Capital I*, p668.

162 MARX, K. *Capital I*, p714.

163 MARX, K. *Capital I*, p724.

164 MARX, K. *Capital I*, p668.

165 MARX, K. *Capital I*, p689.

166 MARX, K. *Capital I*, p668.

167 MARX, K. *Capital I*, p700.

168 MARX, K. *Capital I*, Ch. 28.

169 MARX, K. *Capital I*, p714.

170 MARX, K. *Capital I*, p685.

171 MARX, K. *Capital I*, p689.

172 MARX, K. *Capital I*, p689.

173 MARX, K. *Capital I*, p703.

174 ELSTER, J. *Making Sense of Marx*. Cambridge University

Press, 1985, p429.

175 MARX, K. Guizot, Pouquoi la RévolutionD'Anglterre a-t-elleRéussi? Discours sur le Histoire de la RévolutionD'Angleterre, Paris, 1850. *Neue Rheinische Zeitung*. Politisch-ökonomische Revue. No. 2, 1850. (*MECW Vol. XX*, p254.)

176 ELSTER, J., p429.

177 Elster acknowledges a degree of longevity in the French revolution, noting that the constitutional monarchy is the one established in 1815, not the brief episode after 1789. Yet he (mistakenly) further contracts the revolutionary period in England when he reads Marx's discussion of the 'immediate causes' of the Glorious Revolution of 1688 as an analysis of the causes of the English Revolution.

178 ELSTER, J.(1985), p319.

179 ELSTER, J.(1985), p319-20.

180 MARX, K. *Capital I*, p319.

181 General Regulations on Peasants Emerging from Bondage, 1861.

182 PUSHKAREV, S. *The Emergence of Modern Russia 1801-1917*. Pica Pica Press, 1985, p141.

183 See LYASHCHENKO, P.I., History of the National Economy of Russia to the 1917 Revolution. New York, Octagon Books, 1970, p380-1.

184 Rural Welfare (Landowners Journal), See LYASHCHENKO, P.I.,p381.

185 LYASHCHENKO, P.I., p381.

186 For the purpose of calculating the amount of land which was to pass into the possession of the peasants, the Tsarist regime divided the Russian Empire into three zones, based on the quality of arable land in each area. These zones – the Black Soil region, the Non-Black Soil region and the Steppes – were then further divided into districts by local land commissions and a maximum allotment was set for each

district. The minimum allotment, for the best arable land in each district, was to be one-third of the local maximum. Maximum allotments ranged from 7.4 acres to 16.2 acres in Black Soil districts, 8.1 acres to 18.9 acres in Non-Black Soil districts and 8.1 to 32.4 acres in the Steppe districts.

187 PUSHKAREV, S.,p141, and KEEP,J. Imperial Russia: Alexander II to the Revolution. In AUTY,R. and OBOLENSKY, D. *An Introduction to Russian History*, Cambridge University Press, 1977, p223.

188 At 450-525 kg/ha., arable productivity in mid-nineteenth century Russia equates closely to that attained in England during the fifteenth century, where, as noted by Marx, 4 acres per household was considered sufficient to 'breed a subject to live in convenient plenty...and to keep the plough in the hands of the owners and not mere hirelings'. (Bacon, writing in 1719, about late fifteenth century England, quoted in *Capital I*, p674.) Using average figures for size of allotment (9.1 acres per adult male), productivity, redemption fees (1.5 roubles per dessyatin), and price of rye (1.375 kopeks/lb), the cost of redemption would represent 80 per cent of the output of 1 acre, leaving an average of 8.3 acres per 'soul' to cover seed, subsistence, miscellaneous obligations and soul tax. (Note that the English peasant of the fifteenth century was also subject to a range of miscellaneous obligations and taxes, even when free from a state of villeinage.)
Productivity figures for Russia calculated from LYASHCHENKO, P.I., p324, for England, from CLARK,G. Yields Per Acre in English Agriculture 1250-1860: Evidence from Labour Inputs. *Economic History Review* XLIV, 3, 1991., p445-460, OVERTON,M. *Agricultural Revolution in England – The Transformation of the Agrarian Economy 1500-1850.* Cambridge University Press, 1996, p77. Price of rye from PUSHKAREV, S., p210.

189 LYASHCHENKO, P.I., p418. Serfs of estate-less nobles:

12,000, in manorial factories: 59,000, in state factories and mills: 386,000, in state mines: 230,000, in private mills: 519,000, on petty-estates who received no land allotment: 137,000 and domestic and monthly workers: 1,461,000.

190 LYASHCHENKO, P.I., p419.

191 It is important to note that while land allocations were calculated 'per soul' (adult male), lands were allocated to households, not individual members. Thus, many households received more than one allotment.

192 That is, as plots of insufficient size to save their possessors from proletarian wagelabour.

193 KEEP, J., p224.

194 PUSHKAREV, S., p214 and KEEP, J., p224.

195 By 1907, 1,319,000 peasant families had purchased 22,320,000 acres with the aid of the Peasant Land Bank.

196 PUSHKAREV, S., p208.

197 KEEP, J., p224. A further 15.2 million acres was cultivated by peasants under a miscellany of local agreements which defied categorisation as allotment, private or leased land.

198 1905 Agrarian Census, see LYASHCHENKO, P.I., p739. Peasant allotment distribution by percentage of households: 1-4 dessyatin (2.7-10.8 acres): 15.8 per cent, 4-8 dessyatin (10.8-21.6): 33.7 per cent, 8-20 dessyatin (21.6-54): 10.5 per cent. Distribution by percentage of land held: 3.6 per cent, 19 per cent, 41.8 per cent, 35.6 per cent.

199 Pushkarev gives unreferenced figures for 1905 which suggest that 76.2 per cent of peasant households cultivated more than 13.5 acres of allotment land.

200 ROBINSON, G.T. *Rural Russia Under the Old Regime* Macmillan, 1932., p192.

201 Pre-1870 yield estimates from LYASHCHENKO, P.I., p324, 1905 yield based on a 10-year average (1900-1910), from MITCHELL, B.R. *International Historical Statistics – Europe 1750-1988* (3rd ed.) Macmillan,1992, p239 & 295.

202 See ROBINSON, G.T., p241.

203 LYASHCHENKO, P.I., p751.

204 ROBINSON, G.T., p236.

205 LYASHCHENKO, P.I., p750.

206 LYASHCHENKO, P.I., p750.

207 The studies of 1910-1912, referred to above, found that of a total of 105,594 households, only 3235 (3.06 per cent) hired term workers, at an average of 1.25 workers per hiring household, or one agricultural wage labourer per 25 households all told.

208 PUSHKAREV, S., p143.

209 ROBINSON, G.T., p76.

210 ROBINSON, G.T., p76.

211 Which by this time included the lands occupied by the former state peasants who had been converted to the status of redemption paying peasants in 1886.

212 SEATON-WATSON, H. The Decline of Imperial Russia 1855-1914. Methuen, 1952, p1.

213 This is a generous estimate. The studies concerned were made in four provinces, all in relatively advanced and productive regions. Robinson suggests that reports from most regions of the Empire indicated 'only a very limited development of permanent or semi-permanent wage labour in agriculture' (p240).

214 *Istoryia VKP (b)* p7. (From LYASHCHENKO, P.I., p548.)

215 LYASHCHENKO, P.I., p545.

216 KEEP,J., p222. Using RASHIN, A. G. *Formirovaniyeraboche-goklassa Rossi* (Moscow, 1958).

217 MILIUTIN, V.P. *The Agricultural Workers and the War.* Petrograd, 1917.

218 ROGGER, H., p112.

219 EDELMAN, R. *Gentry Politics on the Eve of the Russian Revolution.* New Brunswick: Rutgers University Press,1980, p15.

220 EDELMAN, R., p16.

221 EDELMAN, R., p17.

222 IASNOPOLSKII, M., in *Mir Bozhii,* December 1903.

223 EDELMAN, R., p16-17.

224 EDELMAN, R., p17.

225 EDELMAN, R., p17-19.

226 ROGGER, H., p90.

227 WALKIN, J. *The Rise of Democracy in Pre-Revolutionary Russia*. Thames and Hudson, 1963, p.107-8.

228 PUSHKAREV, S., p222.

229 KEEP, J., p217.

230 KEEP, J., p221.

231 1 verst=0.66 miles.

232 SEATON-WATSON, H., p115-16.

233 KEEP, J., p218.

234 SEATON-WATSON, H., p117.

235 SEATON-WATSON, H., p284.

236 LYASHCHENKO, P.I., p719.

237 LYASHCHENKO, P.I., p719.

238 LYASHCHENKO, P.I., p687.

239 LYASHCHENKO, P.I., p704.

240 KEEP, J., p220.

241 While, on the one hand, the government was able to strengthen its position at a time of crisis with an 850 million rouble loan from an international consortium in 1906, on the other hand, its budgetary options were limited by 2.6 billion roubles of foreign debt by 1914. (From 1900, around 20 per cent of government expenditure was spent on amortisation of foreign debt.) KEEP,J., p220-221.

242 MARX, K. *Capital I*, p714.

243 MARX, K. *Capital I*, p714.

244 MARX, K. *Capital I*, p714.

245 NOVE, A. *Studies in Economics and Russia*. Macmillan, 1990, p46.

246 NOVE, A. (1990), p46.

247 NOVE, A. (1990), p43.

248 The decree became law in February 1918.

249 LENIN, V.I. *Collected Works* Vol 25. Lawrence and Wishart, 1962, p69.

250 BUKHARIN and PREOBRAZHENSKY *Azbuka Komunizma* (1919), p195-96. (Quoted in NOVE,A. *An Economic History of the USSR*. (2nd ed.) Penguin, 1989.)

251 ENGELS, F. *The Peasant Question in France and Germany*. 1894 See MARX, K. and ENGELS,F. *Selected Works* Vol. 2. Lawrence and Wishart, 1950, p393-4.

252 CONQUEST, R. *Agricultural Workers in the USSR*. Bodley Head, 1968, p14-15.

253 NOVE, A. (1990), p47.

254 NOVE, A (1989), p39.

255 NOVE, A (1989), p39.

256 WILES, R. *Political Economy and Socialism*. Oxford: Blackwell, 1963.

257 DOBB, M. *Russian Economic Development since the Revolution*. Routledge, 1928, p49.

258 KRITSMAN, L.N. *VKA* No. 9, p105. See NOVE,A (1989), p70.

259 FIRSOV, V. *VSA* No.2, 1923. See NOVE, A (1989), p70.

260 LARIN, Yu. *VSA*No. 6, 1924. See NOVE, A (1989), p71.

261 KRITSMAN, L.N. *VKA* No. 9, p105. See NOVE, A (1989), p52-3.

262 LENIN, V.I. Vol. XLII, p193.

263 NOVE, A. (1990), p58.

264 NOVE, A. (1989), p74.

265 Quoted in SUNY, R.G. *The Soviet Experiment – Russia, the USSR and the Successor States*. Oxford University Press, 1998, p136.

266 LENIN, V.I. *Collected Works* Vol XXXII. Lawrence and Wishart, 1962, p185.

267 McCAULEY, M. The Soviet Union 1917-1991 (2nd ed.) Longman, 1993, p48.

268 LENIN, V.I. Vol. XXXII p215. Note that Lenin is not here suggesting that agreement with the peasantry could save the revolution *as an alternative* to foreign revolutions, but *until* such revolutions occur. Elsewhere in the same speech, Lenin is clear that, ultimately, the Bolshevik revolution could only succeed with support from communist revolutionary regimes in the advanced countries (see below).

269 LENIN, V.I. Vol. XXXII, p224.

270 LENIN, V.I. Vol. XXXII, p214.

271 NOVE, A. (1990), p60.

272 LENIN, V.I. op. cit., Vol. 32, p215.

273 Quoted in D'ENCAUSSE, H.C. Lenin – Revolution and Power. Longman,1982, p137.

274 NOVE, A. op. cit. (1990), p60.

275 D'ENCAUSSE, H.C. op. cit., p133.

276 While the Bolsheviks viewed such processes as a tactical retreat to the capitalism of the pre-revolutionary era, I have argued that Tsarist Russia cannot be regarded as capitalist, and was significantly feudal in character. These processes are therefore viewed here as part of the forward transition from feudalism to capitalism.

277 McCAULEY, M, p57, NOVE, A. (1989), p96.

278 NOVE, A. (1989), p96.

279 NOVE, A. (1989), p99.

280 Gladkov (See NOVE, A. (1989), p98).

281 McCAULEY, M. NOVE, A. (1989). McCauley gives the number of kulak households in 1927 variously as 750,000, or 3.4 per cent (p71) and 1 million, or 3.9 per cent (p58). Nove quotes Polyanski's estimate of 7 per cent (p102). Many of the 'employing households' actually employed labour for only a month or so a year.

282 D'ENCAUSSE, H.C., p132, NOVE, A. (1989), p76.

283 NOVE, A. (1989), p84, 102, 176.

284 LENIN, V.I. Vol.33, p424.

285 From 105 million hectares in 1913 to 110.3 in 1926.

286 Lewin, quoted in NOVE, A. (1989), p97.

287 D'ENCAUSSE, H.C., p135 says 77.5 per cent of industrial workers received their wages in kind in 1921, NOVE, A. (1989) p103 says 93.2 per cent in 1921, 50 per cent in 1922 and 20 per cent in 1923.

288 Over 98 per cent of heavy industry was directly controlled by the state in 1922 – NOVE, A. (1989), p94.

289 NOVE, A. (1989), p93.

290 NOVE, A. (1989), p94.

291 LENIN, V.I. Vol XXXIII, p96.

292 From NOVE, A. (1989), p93 & 94 and CARR, E.H and DAVIES, R.W. *Foundations of a Planned Economy 1926-1929* Vol. 1. Part II. Macmillan, 1969, p950 & 961.

293 D'ENCAUSSE, H.C, p134.

294 From NOVE, A. (1989), p93 & 83.

295 NOVE, A. (1989), p93 & 83.

296 NOVE, A. (1989), p90.

297 NOVE, A. (1989), p134-5.

298 NOVE, A. (1989), p134.

299 LENIN, V.I. Vol.XXXIII, p470. Lenin suggested that 'We might, with luck, go through this epoch in ten or twenty years.'

300 NOVE, A. (1989), p80.

301 DOBB, M. *Soviet Economic Development Since 1917* (6th ed.) Routledge & Keegan Paul, 1966, p311.

302 The urban population in 1926 amounted to 18 per cent of the total population of 147 million; in 1913 that group had represented 18 per cent of a total population of 166 million. Figures from WESTWOOD, J.N. *Endurance and Endeavour – Russian History 1812-1980.* (2nd ed.) Oxford University Press, 1981.

303 MITCHELL, B.R. *International Historical Statistics – Europe 1750-1988* (3rd ed.) Macmillan, 1992, p416-457.

304 DOBB, M., p179.

305 DOBB, M., p178.

306 Stalin's speech to the Fifteenth Party Congress, December 1927.

307 Stalin legitimised his tactics with reference to Article 107 of the criminal code, under which the authorities could regard possession of grain as 'hoarding for a speculative purpose' and confiscate stocks without payment.

308 Address to students at the Sverdlov Communist University. See WARD, C. *Stalin's Russia* (2nd ed.) Arnold,1999, p153.

309 WARD, C., p154.

310 Land productivity grew more slowly than labour productivity, reflecting the Soviet policy of bringing marginal lands under cultivation, as well as the focus on the mechanisation of agriculture through larger scale farming and the development of the network of Machine Tractor Stations from the late 1920s.
     Calculations are from the following sources: UK sown area 1850, 15.3m acres (6.12m ha) OVERTON, M. (1996), p76; UK agricultural workforce 1850, 1.1m OVERTON, M. (1996), p126; UK wheat productivity 1850, 23bsh/ac (1748 kg/ha), OVERTON, M. (1996), p77. USSR sown area 1939, 92m ha (227m acres) SUHARA, M. *Russian Agricultural Statistics.* Hitotsubashi University Press, 2017. USSR agricultural workforce 1939, 13.5m SUHARA, M. (2017). USSR grain output 1939, 95.6 million tons, and productivity 8.6 tons/ha (1055kg/ha) NOVE,A. 1989, p268

311 BECKER, C et al. *Russian Urbanisation in the Soviet and Post-Soviet Eras.* IIED, 2012.

312 SANDLE, M. *A Short History of Soviet Socialismi.*UCL Press, 1999, p229.

313 NOVE, A. (1989) p333 and p371.

314 *Novyi Mir* 1986. No. 12.

315 WHITE, S. *After Gorbachev*. Cambridge University Press, 1993.

316 SUNY, R.G. (1998), p451.

317 SUNY, R.G. (1998), p453.

318 https://www.dailymail.co.uk/news/article-5693381/Karl-Marx-titan-terror-communist-ideology-murdered-millions.html

319 https://www.youtube.com/watch?v=GfEYKSxXC5o and https://www.youtube.com/watch?v=jYxvRtDiOjQ Peterson now also claims that Nietzsche 'foretold specifically' in *The Will to Power* 'that 100 million people would die because of the rise of communist ideas'. (Peterson makes this claim here https://www.youtube.com/watch?v=iRPDGEgaATU) Good luck finding that prediction. Maybe he means the bit where Nietzsche says that socialism can't work and an experiment with socialism would be worthwhile in order to prove him right 'even if it were accomplished only by a vast expenditure of lives' because 'the earth is big enough and man is still unexhausted enough'. OK then – so it's fine if a vast number of people die, because there are lots of spare people around, it's not like we'll run out or anything. NIETZSCHE, F. *The Will to Power*. Foulis, 1914, p103.

320 SNYDER, Bloodlands: Europe between Hitler and Stalin. New York, 2010.

321 CONQUEST, R. Excess Deaths in the Soviet Union, *New Left Review*. October 1996. Conquest inflates his initial estimate based on his assumption that the Soviet population *should* have grown by 3 million per year from 1926 to 1937, despite growth of only 1.8 million per year between 1920 and 1926 – a period of recovery from civil war, in which unusually rapid growth might have been expected. https://newleftreview.org/issues/I219/articles/robert-conquest-excess-deaths-in-the-soviet-union.

Works Cited

BECKER, C et al. *Russian Urbanisation in the Soviet and Post-Soviet Eras*. IIED, 2012.

CARR, E.H and DAVIES, R.W. *Foundations of a Planned Economy 1926-1929* Vol. 1. Part II. Macmillan 1969.

CLARK, G. Yields Per Acre in English Agriculture 1250-1860: Evidence from Labour Inputs. *Economic History Review* XLIV, 3, 1991.

COHEN, G.A. *Karl Marx's Theory of History – A Defence*. Princeton University Press, 1976, and 2nd ed. 2000.

COHEN, G.A. Functional Explanation: Reply to Elster. *Political Studies* Vol.XXVIII, No.1. 1980.

COHEN, G.A. Reply to Elster on 'Marxism, Functionalism and Game Theory'. In CALLLINICOS,A.(ed.) *Marxist Theory*. Oxford University Press, 1989.

CONQUEST, R. *Agricultural Workers in the USSR*. Bodley Head, 1968.

CONQUEST, R. Excess Deaths in the Soviet Union, *New Left Review*. October 1996.

D'ENCAUSSE, H.C. *Lenin – Revolution and Power*. Longman,1982.

DOBB,M. *Russian Economic Development since the Revolution*. Routledge, 1928.

DOBB, M. *Soviet Economic Development Since 1917* (6th ed.) Routledge & Keegan Paul, 1966.

EDELMAN, R. *Gentry Politics on the Eve of the Russian Revolution*. New Brunswick: Rutgers University Press,1980.

ELSTER,J. *Making Sense of Marx*. Cambridge University Press, 1985.

ELSTER, J. Further thoughts on Marxism, functionalism and game theory in ROEMER,J. *Analytical Marxism* Cambridge University Press, 1986.

ENGELS, F. *The Peasant Question in France and Germany*, 1894.

ENGELS, F.*The Origin of the Family, Private Property and the State.* New York, 1942.

FUKUYAMA, F. Marxism's Failure. *The Independent,* 21.9.89.

FUKUYAMA, F *The End of History and the Last Man.* Penguin, 1992.

HILTON, R.H. (ed.) *The Transition from Feudalism to Capitalism.* New Left Books, 1976.

HODGES, D. The Intermediate Classes in Marxian Theory. *Social Research,* 23, 1961.

KEEP, J. Imperial Russia: Alexander II to the Revolution. In AUTY, R. and OBOLENSKY, D. *An Introduction to Russian History,* Cambridge University Press, 1977.

KLEBNIKOV, P.G. *Agricultural Development in Russia, 1906-17: Land Reform, Social Agronomy and Cooperation,* 1991.

KNEI-PAZ, R. *The Social and Political Thought of Leon Trotsky.* Oxford University Press, 1978.

KOSMINSKY, E.A. *Studies in the Agrarian History of England in the Thirteenth Century.* Oxford: Basil Blackwell, 1956.

LENIN,V.I. 'Report on the Unity Congress of the RSDLP – A Letter to the St. Petersburg Workers'. May/June 1906.

LENIN, V.I. *Collected Works,* Lawrence and Wishart, 1962 (Volumes 10, 25, 32, 33, 42).

LYASHCHENKO, P.I. *History of the National Economy of Russia to the 1917 Revolution,* New York, Octagon Books, 1970.

MARX, K. *Deutsche-Brüsseler-Zeitung* No. 92, November 18 1847.

MARX, K. Guizot, Pouquoi la RévolutionD'Anglterre a-t-elleRéussi? Discours sur le Histoire de la RévolutionD'Angleterre, Paris, 1850. *Neue Rheinische Zeitung.* Politisch-ökonomische Revue. No. 2, 1850.

MARX, K. *Capital I.* Lawrence and Wishart, 1954.

MARX, K. *Capital II* Lawrence and Wishart,1956.

MARX, K. *Capital III.* Lawrence and Wishart, 1959.

MARX, K. *Pre-Capitalist Economic Formations.* Lawrence and Wishart,1964.

MARX, K. *Grundrisse.* Penguin, 1973.

MARX, K. *The Poverty of Philosophy* Moscow: Progress Publishers, 1975.

MARX, K. *Preface and Introduction to A Contribution to the Critique of Political Economy.* (1859) Peking: Foreign Languages Press, 1976.

MARX, K *and* ENGELS, F. *Collected Works.* Lawrence and Wishart, 1975 (Volumes 5, 6, 20, 24, 34).

MARX, K. and ENGELS, F. *Selected Works* Vol. 2. Lawrence and Wishart, 1950.

McCAULEY, M. *The Soviet Union 1917-1991* (2nd ed.) Longman, 1993.

McLENNAN, G. *Marxism and the Methodologies of History.* Verso, 1981.

MILIUTIN, V.P. *The Agricultural Workers and the War.* Petrograd, 1917.

MITCHELL, B.R. *International Historical Statistics – Europe 1750-1988* (3rd ed.) Macmillan, 1992.

NIETZSCHE, F. *The Will to Power.* Foulis, 1914.

NOVE, A. *An Economic History of the USSR.* (2nd ed.) Penguin, 1989.

NOVE, A. *Studies in Economics and Russia* Macmillan, 1990.

OVERTON, M. *Agricultural Revolution in England – The Transformation of the Agrarian Economy 1500-1850.* Cambridge University Press, 1996.

PILGER, J. 'How Thatcher Gave Pol Pot a Hand' in the *New Statesman,* 17 April 2000.

PLEKHANOV, G.V. *The Development of the Monist View of History.* Moscow, 1972.

POULANTZAS, N. *Classes in Contemporary Capitalism.* New Left Books, 1975.

PUSHKAREV, S. *The Emergence of Modern Russia 1801-1917.* Pica Pica Press, 1985.

RIGBY, S.H. *Marxism and History – A Critical Introduction.*

Manchester University Press, 1987.

ROEMER, J. New Directions in the Marxian Theory of Exploitation and Class. *Politics and Society*, vol.11, no. 3, 1982.

ROBINSON, G.T. *Rural Russia Under the Old Regime* Macmillan, 1932.

SANDLE, M. *A Short History of Soviet Socialism* UCL Press, 1999.

SEATON-WATSON, H. The *Decline of Imperial Russia 1855-1914*. Methuen, 1952.

SHANIN, T. (ed.) *Late Marx and the Russian Road*. Routledge,1984.

SNYDER, *Bloodlands: Europe between Hitler and Stalin*. New York, 2010.

SUHARA, M. *Russian Agricultural Statistics*. Hitotsubashi University Press, 2017.

SUNY, R.G. *The Soviet Experiment – Russia, the USSR and the Successor States*. Oxford University Press, 1998.

THOMPSON, E.P. *The Making of the English Working Class*. Penguin, 1968.

THOMPSON, E.P. *The Poverty of Theory and other Essays*. Merlin, 1978.

VINOGRADOFF, P. *Villainage in England – Essays in English Mediaeval History*. Oxford University Press, 1968.

WALKIN, J. *The Rise of Democracy in Pre-Revolutionary Russia*. Thames and Hudson, 1963.

WARD, C. *Stalin's Russia* (2nd ed.) Arnold, 1999.

WESTWOOD, J.N. *Endurance and Endeavour – Russian History 1812-1980*. (2nd ed.) Oxford University Press, 198.

WHITE, S. *After Gorbachev* Cambridge University Press, 1993.

WILES, R. *Political Economy and Socialism*. Oxford: Blackwell, 1963.

WRIGHT, E.O. *Class, Crisis and the State*. New Left Books, 1978.

WRIGHT, E.O. What is Middle About the Middle Class? In ROEMER, J. (ed) *Analytical Marxism*. Cambridge University Press, 1986.

CULTURE, SOCIETY & POLITICS

The modern world is at an impasse. Disasters scroll across our smartphone screens and we're invited to like, follow or upvote, but critical thinking is harder and harder to find. Rather than connecting us in common struggle and debate, the internet has sped up and deepened a long-standing process of alienation and atomization. Zer0 Books wants to work against this trend. With critical theory as our jumping off point, we aim to publish books that make our readers uncomfortable. We want to move beyond received opinions.

Zer0 Books is on the left and wants to reinvent the left. We are sick of the injustice, the suffering and the stupidity that defines both our political and cultural world, and we aim to find a new foundation for a new struggle.

If this book has helped you to clarify an idea, solve a problem or extend your knowledge, you may want to check out our online content as well. Look for Zer0 Books: Advancing Conversations in the iTunes directory and for our Zer0 Books YouTube channel.

Popular videos include:

Žižek and the Double Blackmain

The Intellectual Dark Web is a Bad Sign

Can there be an Anti-SJW Left?

Answering Jordan Peterson on Marxism

Follow us on Facebook
at https://www.facebook.com/ZeroBooks and Twitter at https://
twitter.com/Zer0Books

Bestsellers from Zer0 Books include:

Give Them An Argument
Logic for the Left
Ben Burgis
Many serious leftists have learned to distrust talk of logic. This is
a serious mistake.
Paperback: 978-1-78904-210-8 ebook: 978-1-78904-211-5

Poor but Sexy
Culture Clashes in Europe East and West
Agata Pyzik
How the East stayed East and the West stayed West.
Paperback: 978-1-78099-394-2 ebook: 978-1-78099-395-9

An Anthropology of Nothing in Particular
Martin Demant Frederiksen
A journey into the social lives of meaninglessness.
Paperback: 978-1-78535-699-5 ebook: 978-1-78535-700-8

In the Dust of This Planet
Horror of Philosophy vol. 1
Eugene Thacker
In the first of a series of three books on the Horror of Philosophy,
In the Dust of This Planet offers the genre of horror as a way of
thinking about the unthinkable.
Paperback: 978-1-84694-676-9 ebook: 978-1-78099-010-1

The End of Oulipo?
An Attempt to Exhaust a Movement
Lauren Elkin, Veronica Esposito
Paperback: 978-1-78099-655-4 ebook: 978-1-78099-656-1

Capitalist Realism
Is There no Alternative?
Mark Fisher
An analysis of the ways in which capitalism has presented itself
as the only realistic political-economic system.
Paperback: 978-1-84694-317-1 ebook: 978-1-78099-734-6

Rebel Rebel
Chris O'Leary
David Bowie: every single song. Everything you want to know,
everything you didn't know.
Paperback: 978-1-78099-244-0 ebook: 978-1-78099-713-1

Kill All Normies
Angela Nagle
Online culture wars from 4chan and Tumblr to Trump.
Paperback: 978-1- 78535-543-1 ebook: 978-1-78535-544-8

Cartographies of the Absolute
Alberto Toscano, Jeff Kinkle
An aesthetics of the economy for the twenty-first century.
Paperback: 978-1-78099-275-4 ebook: 978-1-78279-973-3

Malign Velocities
Accelerationism and Capitalism
Benjamin Noys
Long listed for the Bread and Roses Prize 2015, *Malign Velocities*
argues against the need for speed, tracking acceleration
as the symptom of the ongoing crises of capitalism.
Paperback: 978-1-78279-300-7 ebook: 978-1-78279-299-4

Meat Market
Female Flesh under Capitalism
Laurie Penny
A feminist dissection of women's bodies as the fleshy fulcrum of
capitalist cannibalism, whereby women are both consumers and
consumed.
Paperback: 978-1-84694-521-2 ebook: 978-1-84694-782-7

Babbling Corpse
Vaporwave and the Commodification of Ghosts
Grafton Tanner
Paperback: 978-1-78279-759-3 ebook: 978-1-78279-760-9

New Work New Culture
Work we want and a culture that strengthens us
Frithjoff Bergmann
A serious alternative for mankind and the planet.
Paperback: 978-1-78904-064-7 ebook: 978-1-78904-065-4

Romeo and Juliet in Palestine
Teaching Under Occupation
Tom Sperlinger
Life in the West Bank, the nature of pedagogy and the role of a
university under occupation.
Paperback: 978-1-78279-637-4 ebook: 978-1-78279-636-7

Ghosts of My Life
Writings on Depression, Hauntology and Lost Futures
Mark Fisher
Paperback: 978-1-78099-226-6 ebook: 978-1-78279-624-4

Sweetening the Pill
or How We Got Hooked on Hormonal Birth Control
Holly Grigg-Spall
Has contraception liberated or oppressed women?
Sweetening the Pill breaks the silence on the dark side of hormonal
contraception.
Paperback: 978-1-78099-607-3 ebook: 978-1-78099-608-0

Why Are We The Good Guys?
Reclaiming your Mind from the Delusions of Propaganda
David Cromwell
A provocative challenge to the standard ideology that Western
power is a benevolent force in the world.
Paperback: 978-1-78099-365-2 ebook: 978-1-78099-366-9

The Writing on the Wall
On the Decomposition of Capitalism and its Critics
Anselm Jappe, Alastair Hemmens
A new approach to the meaning of social emancipation.
Paperback: 978-1-78535-581-3 ebook: 978-1-78535-582-0

Enjoying It
Candy Crush and Capitalism
Alfie Bown
A study of enjoyment and of the enjoyment of studying. Bown asks what enjoyment says about us and what we say about enjoyment, and why.
Paperback: 978-1-78535-155-6 ebook: 978-1-78535-156-3

Color, Facture, Art and Design
Iona Singh
This materialist definition of fine-art develops guidelines for architecture, design, cultural-studies and ultimately social change.
Paperback: 978-1-78099-629-5 ebook: 978-1-78099-630-1

Neglected or Misunderstood
The Radical Feminism of Shulamith Firestone
Victoria Margree
An interrogation of issues surrounding gender, biology, sexuality, work and technology, and the ways in which our imaginations continue to be in thrall to ideologies of maternity and the nuclear family.
Paperback: 978-1-78535-539-4 ebook: 978-1-78535-540-0

How to Dismantle the NHS in 10 Easy Steps (Second Edition)
Youssef El-Gingihy
The story of how your NHS was sold off and why you will have to buy private health insurance soon. A new expanded second edition with chapters on junior doctors' strikes and government blueprints for US-style healthcare.
Paperback: 978-1-78904-178-1 ebook: 978-1-78904-179-8

Digesting Recipes
The Art of Culinary Notation
Susannah Worth
A recipe is an instruction, the imperative tone of the expert, but this constraint can offer its own kind of potential. A recipe need not be a domestic trap but might instead offer escape – something to fantasise about or aspire to.
Paperback: 978-1-78279-860-6 ebook: 978-1-78279-859-0

Most titles are published in paperback and as an ebook.
Paperbacks are available in traditional bookshops. Both print and ebook formats are available online.
Follow us on Facebook
at https://www.facebook.com/ZeroBooks
and Twitter at https://twitter.com/Zer0Books